SMP interact

Book 7T

CAMBRIDGE
UNIVERSITY PRESS

PUBLISHED BY THE PRESS SYNDICATE OF THE UNIVERSITY OF CAMBRIDGE
The Pitt Building, Trumpington Street, Cambridge, United Kingdom

CAMBRIDGE UNIVERSITY PRESS
The Edinburgh Building, Cambridge CB2 2RU, UK
40 West 20th Street, New York, NY 10011-4211, USA
477 Williamstown Road, Port Melbourne, VIC 3207, Australia
Ruiz de Alarcón 13, 28014 Madrid, Spain
Dock House, The Waterfront, Cape Town 8001, South Africa

http://www.cambridge.org/

Printed in the United Kingdom at the University Press, Cambridge

Typeface Minion   *System* QuarkXPress®

A catalogue record for this book is available from the British Library

ISBN 0 521 53797 5 paperback

Typesetting and technical illustrations by The School Mathematics Project, Eikon Illustration
and Jeff Edwards
Illustrations on page 4 by Matthew Soley
Other illustrations by Robert Calow and Steve Lach at Eikon Illustration
Cover image Getty Images/Randy Allbritton
Cover design by Angela Ashton

The publishers thank the following for supplying photographs:
Page 49 London Transport Museum
Page 106 David Bromley
Page 107 John Ling
Page 118 GreatBuildings.com (*left*, Habitat '67 © Artifice Inc.; *right*, Guggenheim Museum,
Bilbao © Lawrence A. Martin)
Page 132 © Charles O'Rear/CORBIS
Page 211 Colin Benwell
Page 218 William Ervin/Science Photo Library (Zebra and Hippo), Wayne Lawler/Science
Photo Library (Kangaroo), Tim Davis/Science Photo Library (Tiger)
Page 237 © Rufus F. Folkks/CORBIS

Logo on page 35 (question C2 (j)) courtesy of National Westminster Bank; catalogue spread on
page 210 courtesy of Littlewood's

Contents

① First bites

A Spot the mistake

You need sheets 45 and 46.

Each picture contains errors.
Some are mathematical, some are not.

How many can you find?

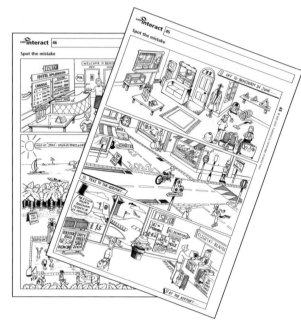

B Four digits

The class chooses four digits, for example

$$1, \ 2, \ 3, \ 4$$

Try to make as many numbers from 1 to 100 as possible.
Use the four digits and any signs you want.

$$1 + 2 + 3 + 4 = \mathbf{10}$$

$$13 + 4 - 2 = \mathbf{15}$$

C 4U + 1T

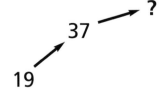

- Continue the 'chain'.
- Start with a different number.
  What happens?
- Try starting with other numbers.

D Finding your way

D1 Jo is walking along Wood Street from the Railway Bridge.
Is Beech Avenue on her left or right?

D2 Sam leaves his house and walks towards Wood Street.
When he reaches Wood Street does he go left or right to go to the Clock Tower?

D3 Nikki leaves her house and walks towards Wood Street.
When she reaches Wood Street which way does she turn to go to the Clock Tower?

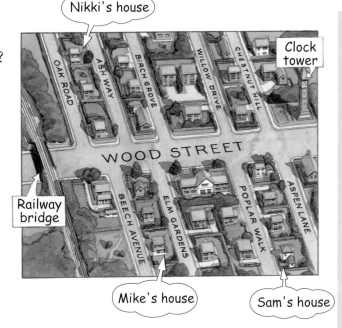

D4 Start at the railway bridge and go along Wood Street.
Oak Road is the **first turning** on your left.
We say **first left**.

Which turnings are these?

(a) Ash Way   (b) Beech Avenue   (c) Poplar Walk

(d) Chestnut Hill   (e) Aspen Lane

D5 Start at the clock tower. Go along Wood Street towards the railway bridge.

(a) Which is the first turning on your left?

(b) Which is the third right?

(c) Which turning is Beech Avenue?

D6 Find Mike's house in Beech Avenue.
From Mike's house describe how you would get to Sam's house in Poplar Walk.

D7 From Sam's house, describe how you would get to Nikki's house in Oak Road.

5

D8 Find the pond at the top
of the map.
You start at the pond
and walk along Windy Lane.

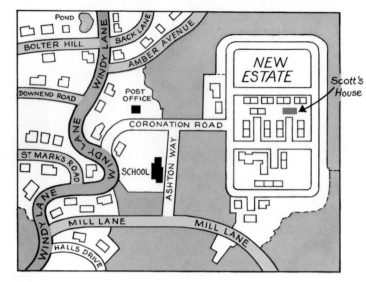

(a) Which is the first
turning on your left?

(b) Which is the second on
your right?

(c) You turn into
Coronation Road. Is the
post office on the left
side or the right side of
the road?

(d) You pass the post office and turn into Ashton Way.
Do you turn left or right?

(e) You walk along Ashton Way.
Is the school on your left or your right?

(f) You stop at Mill Lane, turn round and go back along
Ashton Way.
Which side is the school on, left or right?

D9 You are back by the pond in Windy Lane.
Someone asks you the way to the post office.
What would you say?

D10 Find Scott's house.
The roads on the new estate do not have names yet.
Describe how you would get to Scott's house from the school.

D11 This is a picture of the school.
Which roads can you see in the picture?

E Gridlock

This game is described in the teacher's guide.

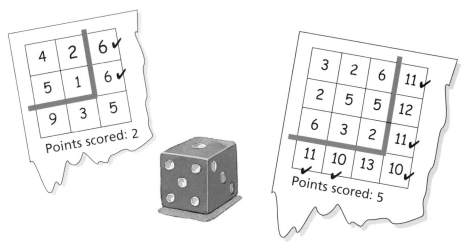

E1 (a) Copy and complete these grids.
Find the points scored for each one.

2		5
3		
	7	

Points scored: ...

		5
	6	9
	7	

Points scored: ...

	6		12
5		1	9
		6	16
	13		10

Points scored: ...

(b) Make up some problems like this for someone else to try.

E2 Tom has made this grid
with 2, 3, 5 and 6.
He has scored 0 points.
Show how he could score
2 points with 2, 3, 5 and 6.

5	2	7
6	3	9
11	5	8

Points scored: 0

E3 In one game, the numbers 6, 4, 3 and 6 were called.
One pupil scored 2 points and one scored 4 points.

With the numbers 6, 4, 3 and 6, show how you could score

(a) 2 points   (b) 4 points

E4 With the numbers 1, 2, 3 and 4,

    (a) what is the highest number of points you can score?

    (b) what is the lowest number of points you can score?

E5 Copy and complete these 'Gridlock' grids.

(a) 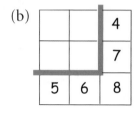   (b)   (c)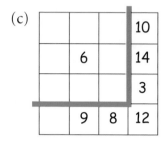

E6 Find a set of four numbers that will always give you a score of 0 points.

E7 Explain why you will always score 5 points with the numbers 1, 2, 2 and 2.

E8 Explain why you will always score some points with the numbers 1, 1, 5 and 2.

E9 Copy and complete these grids.   (a) 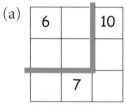   (b)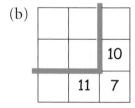

        Points scored: 4   Points scored: 0

E10 With the numbers 1, 2, 2, 3, 4, 5, 5, 6 and 6, show how you could score

    (a) 6 points   (b) 7 points   (c) 0 points

E11 Copy and complete this grid with the numbers 1, 1, 3, 4, 5, 5, 5, 6 and 6.

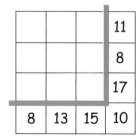

F Patterns from a hexagon

Practise drawing a regular hexagon like this.

1 Set a pair of compasses to about 4 cm apart.

   Draw a circle.

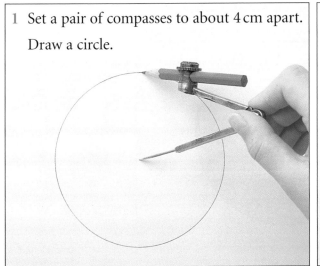

2 Do not change the compasses.
   Put the point anywhere on the circle.

   Make a mark like this.

3 Make another mark like this ...

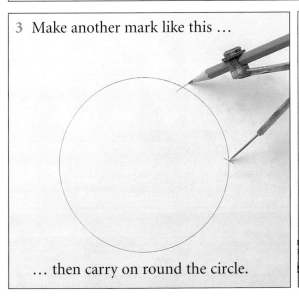

   ... then carry on round the circle.

4 Join the points to draw the hexagon.

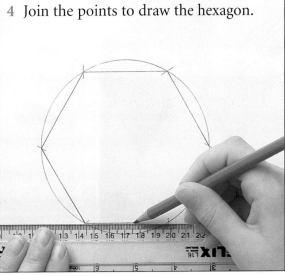

F1 These designs are based on a regular hexagon.
Use the compasses method to help you draw some of them.

Colour your drawings.
Choose your own colours.

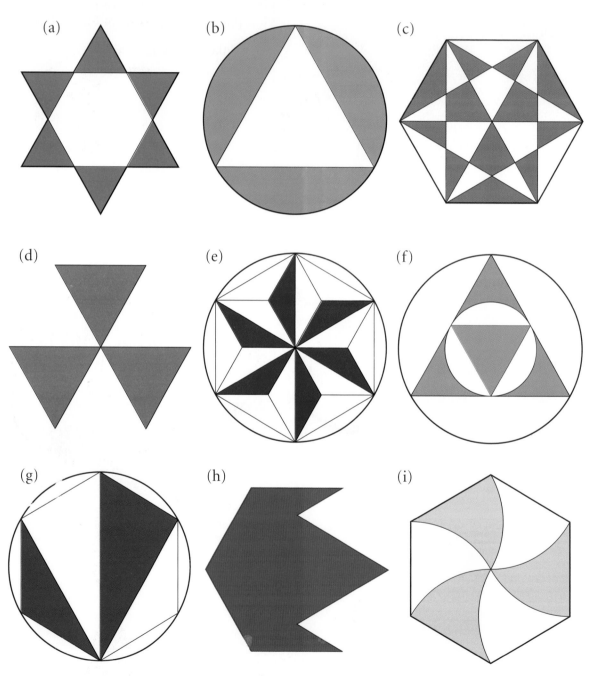

(a)   (b)   (c)

(d)   (e)   (f)

(g)   (h)   (i)

Use compasses to make up designs of your own.

For some patterns you need to draw lines or circles
and then rub parts of them out.

1 Draw a regular
hexagon. Join all the
corners with faint lines.

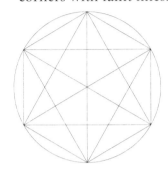

2 Go over these lines
more strongly.

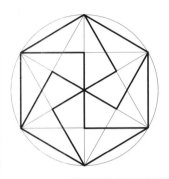

3 Rub out lines you
don't need.
Colour in the pattern.

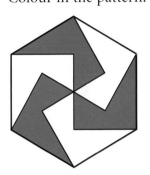

F2 Use the rub-out method to draw some of these.
Colour your drawings.

(a)

(b)

(c)

(d)

(e)

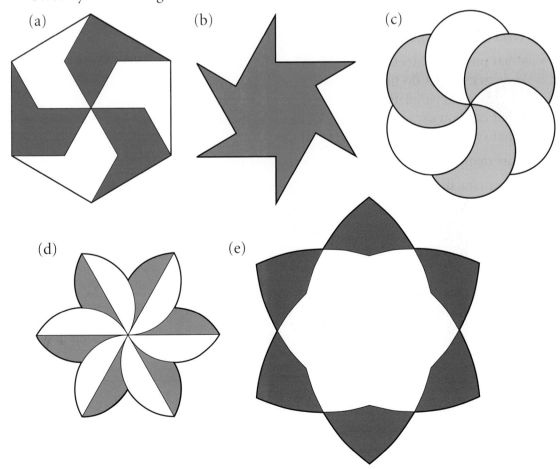

11

G Shapes on a dotty square

These shapes have all been drawn on a 3 by 3 grid.

There are many other shapes that can be drawn.

Rules

- Every corner must be at one of the nine dots.

- These are not allowed:

Draw some shapes of your own on 3 by 3 grids.

- Write down the names of any shapes you know.

- What properties does each of the shapes you have drawn have?
  How many sides do they have?
  Are any sides parallel?
  What can you say about the angles in each of the shapes?
  What symmetry does each of the shapes have?

- How many **different** triangles can you draw on a 3 by 3 grid?

- How many **different** quadrilaterals can you draw on a 3 by 3 grid?

- Can you find the area of any of the shapes you have drawn?

Extensions

How many different shapes can you draw on these grids?

② Number bites

These are short activities to give you regular practice of your number skills.
You don't need to do them all in one bite. Just use each one when you need it.

P Place value

P1 Bigger wins   a game for two players

- Get two sets of 0–9 cards (made from sheet 19).
  Shuffle the pack and
  place it face down.
  Draw a game board like this
  with your own names.

  Make these big enough for a card.

  Bernie   Neeta

- Take turns to pick up a card.
  Put your card in one of your boxes.

  Bernie   Neeta

  | | 4 | | | | | |

- After three turns each you will
  each have a three-digit number.
  The bigger number wins.

  Bernie   Neeta

  | 3 | 4 | 2 | | 5 | 1 | 3 |

Nasty game

When you pick up a card you can put it in one of your opponent's boxes.

P2 Mountains high

These are all the mountains in England
over 3000 feet high.

Write their names in order of height,
highest first.

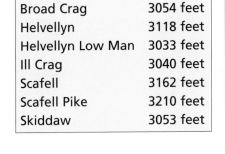

Broad Crag	3054 feet
Helvellyn	3118 feet
Helvellyn Low Man	3033 feet
Ill Crag	3040 feet
Scafell	3162 feet
Scafell Pike	3210 feet
Skiddaw	3053 feet

P3 Oceans deep

These are the deepest oceans and seas.

Write them in order of depth, starting with the least deep.

Name	Greatest depth (metres)
Arctic Ocean	5441
Atlantic Ocean	9219
Bering Sea	4091
Caribbean Sea	7339
Gulf of Mexico	3885
Indian Ocean	8047
Malay Sea	6505
Mediterranean Sea	4400
Pacific Ocean	11 033

A Addition and subtraction

A1 Addition bingo

This activity is described in the teacher's guide.

$8 + 7$

A2 Today's number is ...

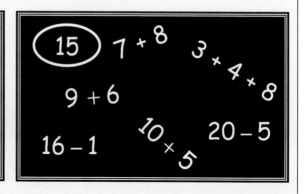

7 $2 + 5$ $6 + 1$

$1 + 6$

$8 - 1$ $10 - 3$

$20 - 13$

15 $7 + 8$ $3 + 4 + 8$

$9 + 6$

$16 - 1$ 10×5 $20 - 5$

A3 Minimal measuring

Here is a set of four strips.

1 cm

3 cm

5 cm

10 cm

You can make different lengths by putting some of the strips end to end like this.

(a) Which strips could you use to make a length of 13 cm?
(You cannot use a strip more than once.)

(b) List all the different lengths you can make
by putting two of these strips end to end.

(c) End to end, what lengths can you make with

(i) three strips   (ii) four strips

(d) Which lengths between 1 cm and 20 cm are
impossible to make with these strips?

(e) Design a set of five strips from which you can make
lengths of 1 cm, 2 cm, 3 cm, … as far up as you can go.

What is the longest length they will make?

A4 Cover up

You need sheet 18.

Cut out the eight rectangular pieces.

Put the pieces on board A.
Each piece should cover a pair of numbers
which add up to give that answer.

For example, 14 may cover 8 and 6, or it
may cover 7 and 7, and so on.

You can use the pieces this way

or this way   .

Now try boards B, C and D.

| 11 | 12 | 13 | 14 |
| 15 | 16 | 17 | 18 |

A

5	8	3	8
9	6	9	7
9	4	8	7
7	9	8	9

Using 2 or 3 pieces: good
4 or 5 pieces: very good
6 or 7 pieces: excellent!
8 pieces: brilliant!

M Multiplication

M1 Today's number is ...

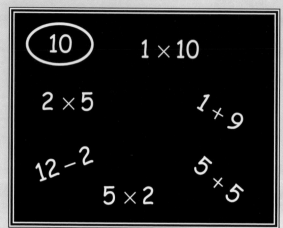

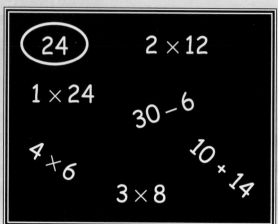

M2 Grids

1 Draw two identical grids of 10 squares.

Write the numbers from 0 to 9, in any order, in one grid.

2	0	6	9	3
7	4	8	1	5

× 6

2 Choose a table you are trying to learn, for example the 6× table.

As quickly as you can, write the answers in the right places in the other grid.

12				

M3 Multiplication dominoes

You need the dominoes made from sheet 29.

Arrange them in a line so that each multiplication matches its answer.

7 × 3	21	4 × 3	12

M4 Multiplication pairs

You need the cards made from sheets 30 to 33.

Play with a partner.
Spread the cards face down on the table.

You turn over two cards.
If they match, you win them.
If not, you turn them back again and your partner has a go.

M5 Links, chains and loops

This is a 'link'.

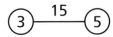

Multiply the numbers in circles
to give the number on the link.

Try copying and completing these links, chains and loops.

(a) ④ —?— ⑦

(b) ? —10— ②

(c) ⑥ —24— ?

(d) ③ —24— ? —32— ?

(e) ? —18— ? —42— ? —35— ⑤

(f)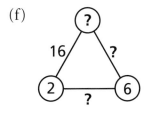

(g)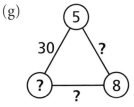

(h)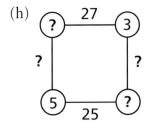

(i)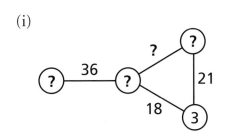

(j)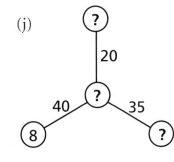

(k)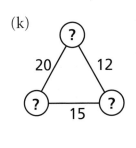

(l)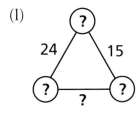

(m)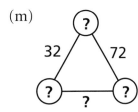

W Work-out – addition, subtraction and multiplication

W1 Three in a line   a game for two players

You need
- a game board (below)
- two dice
- eight counters of one colour and eight counters of another colour

The game

On your turn roll the two dice.

Put a counter on the number you get by

- adding the dice numbers

or
- taking one dice number away from the other

or
- multiplying the dice numbers

Example

You could use

$2 + 5 = \boxed{7}$

or $5 - 2 = \boxed{3}$

or $2 \times 5 = \boxed{10}$

The winner
- The first player with three counters in a line

1	2	3	4
5	●	●	●
9	10	11	12
13	14	15	16

like this

1	●	3	4
5	●	7	8
9	●	11	12
13	14	15	16

or this

1	2	●	4
5	●	7	8
●	10	11	12
13	14	15	16

or this

The game board

1	2	3	4
5	6	7	8
9	10	11	12
13	14	15	16

W2 Pairs   an investigation

- You have the four numbers 2, 3, 5, 7.

  Make them into any two pairs.

  Multiply the numbers in each pair.

  Add the two results together.

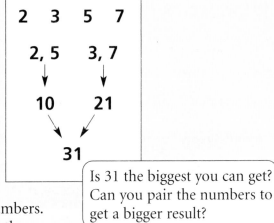

Is 31 the biggest you can get?
Can you pair the numbers to
get a bigger result?

- Investigate for different sets of four numbers.
  Can you find any rules for how to pair the
  numbers to get the largest result?

F Fractions

F1 Shade half, shade a quarter

You need sheet 36 or squared paper.

- A half is written $\frac{1}{2}$.
  Find different ways of shading $\frac{1}{2}$ of this square.
  Here are some suggestions.

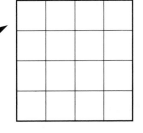

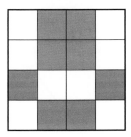
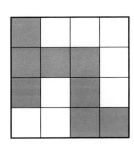

- A quarter is written $\frac{1}{4}$.
  Find different ways of shading $\frac{1}{4}$ of the square.

F2 Naming parts

You need two sheets of paper.

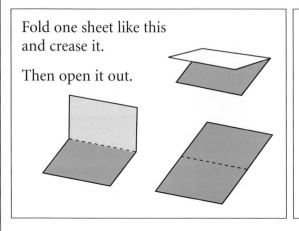

Fold one sheet like this and crease it.

Then open it out.

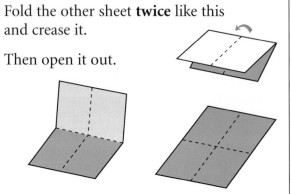

Fold the other sheet **twice** like this and crease it.

Then open it out.

The rest of this activity is described in the teacher's guide.

What name would you give to each of these parts?

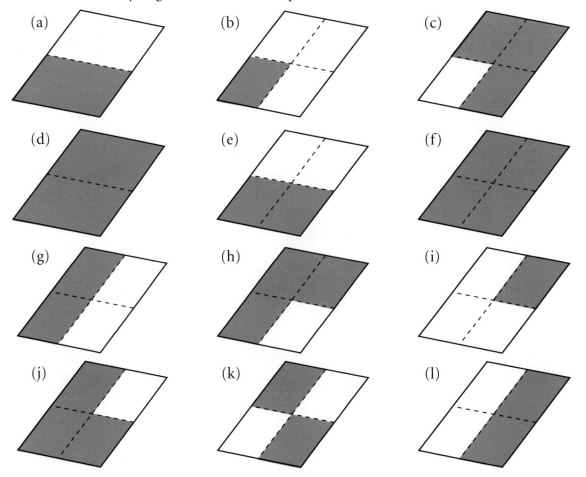

(a)

(b)

(c)

(d)

(e)

(f)

(g)

(h)

(i)

(j)

(k)

(l)

T Time and money

T1 Watch it

A   B   C

D   E   F

G   H   I

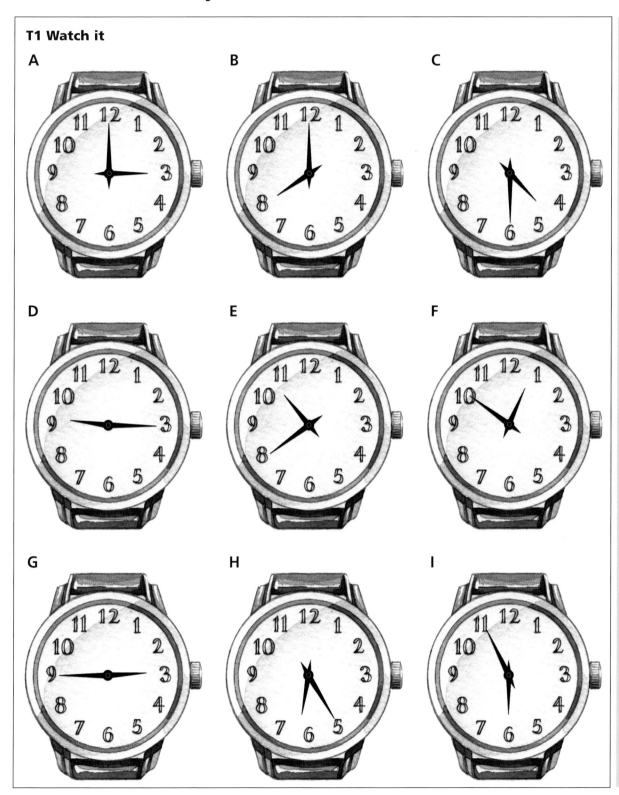

Do these in your head, if you can.

1 Find the change from a £1 coin when you buy

    (a) a Fizzo   (b) a Fudge Finger

    (c) a Fruit Chew   (d) a Tri Bar

    (e) a Moon Bar   (f) a Freshers and a Fizzo

    (g) two Fudge Fingers   (h) a Fruit Chew and an Apple Crunch

2 Find the change from a £5 note when you buy

    (a) an Apple Crunch   (b) two Fizzos

    (c) a Moon Bar and a Freshers   (d) a Fudge Finger and a Fizzo

    (e) two Tri Bars   (f) four Fudge Fingers

3 Kay buys one item with a £1 coin.
   Her change is 95p. What did she buy?

4 Kay buys two items with a £1 coin.
   Her change is 70p. What did she buy?

5 Kay buys two items with a £1 coin.
   Her change is 55p. What did she buy?

*6 Tim buys three items with a £1 coin.
   His change is 6p. What did he buy?

3 Written addition and subtraction

This work will help you

♦ add and subtract numbers without a calculator

♦ investigate patterns involving addition and subtraction

A Written addition practice

Total   a game for three or more players

You need a set of cards numbered 0 to 9 (sheet 19).

- Each player needs to copy the 'Total' grid.
  Draw the grid a bit bigger than here.

- Shuffle the cards and place them
  face down on the table.

- Turn one card over.

- Before the next card is turned over, each player
  must write the digit in an empty space on their grid.
  You cannot change it once it is written down.

- Turn over another card.
  Repeat until all the spaces are filled.

- Each player finds their total.

- The winner is the player with the highest total.

'Total' grid

The first card Amin's
group turned over
was a 7.

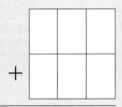

This is how Amin filled
in the rest of his grid.

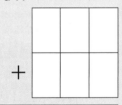

	4	7	2
+	8	5	3
1	3	2	5

His total score was 1325.

Make sure you line up the hundreds, tens and units.

$$45 + 278 \longrightarrow \quad \begin{array}{r} 45 \\ + \underline{278} \\ \underline{323} \\ {\scriptstyle 1\ 1} \end{array}$$

$$158 + 72 \longrightarrow \quad \begin{array}{r} 158 \\ + \underline{72} \\ \underline{230} \\ {\scriptstyle 1\ 1} \end{array}$$

A1 (a) 68 + 127   (b) 246 + 73   (c) 318 + 54   (d) 562 + 118   (e) 409 + 275

A2 (a) 377 + 55   (b) 238 + 94   (c) 197 + 85   (d) 63 + 718   (e) 982 + 38

B Written subtraction practice

Helen is working out 345 − 128.

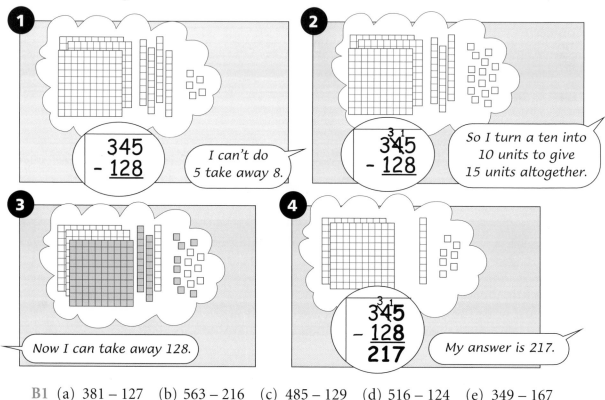

B1 (a) 381 − 127   (b) 563 − 216   (c) 485 − 129   (d) 516 − 124   (e) 349 − 167

B2 (a) 641 − 27   (b) 273 − 36   (c) 347 − 55   (d) 228 − 64   (e) 592 − 77

B3 (a) 625 − 159   (b) 834 − 246   (c) 523 − 48   (d) 747 − 59   (e) 834 − 255

B4 (a) 640 − 217   (b) 570 − 153   (c) 180 − 75   (d) 314 − 70   (e) 320 − 132

B5 (a) 412 − 239   (b) 613 − 258   (c) 913 − 54   (d) 516 − 37   (e) 702 − 51

B6 (a) 301 − 149   (b) 803 − 457   (c) 607 − 139   (d) 503 − 254   (e) 404 − 248

C Money

Make sure you line up the pounds and pence.

$$£2.78 – 47p \longrightarrow £2.78 – £0.47 \longrightarrow \begin{array}{r} £2.78 \\ -\ \underline{£0.47} \\ \underline{£2.31} \end{array}$$

C1 (a) £1.56 + £1.35 (b) £1.74 + £0.28 (c) £1.28 + 43p (d) £2.56 + 63p

C2 (a) £3.67 – £2.25 (b) £2.56 – £1.27 (c) £3.81 – £0.56 (d) £1.63 – 24p

C3 (a) £4.56 – £1.87 (b) £9.24 – £0.57 (c) £4.15 – 68p (d) £10.04 – £7.56

Here is part of the menu from Vallow Tea Rooms.

Vallow Tea Rooms			
Coffee	95p	Blackcurrant ice-cream	£1.55
Tea	80p		
Lemonade	73p	Cheese ploughmans	£3.49
Cola	85p		
		Ham sandwich	£1.50
Scone and jam	95p	Beef sandwich	£1.95
Herb scone	65p	Prawn sandwich	£2.30
Tea cake	75p		

C4 What is the cost of
   (a) a coffee and a herb scone   (b) a tea and a cheese ploughmans
   (c) a lemonade and a blackcurrant ice-cream

C5 How much more does a prawn sandwich cost than a beef sandwich?

C6 Greg bought a tea, a ham sandwich and a tea cake.
   How much change did he get from £5.00?

C7 Asad started with £4.37. He bought a cola and a beef sandwich.
   How much money did he have left?

*C8 Jo's lunch cost £4.44.
   What do you think she had for lunch?

D Investigations

Palindromes

A number palindrome is a number that
does not change when the digits are reversed.

55   141   202   2332

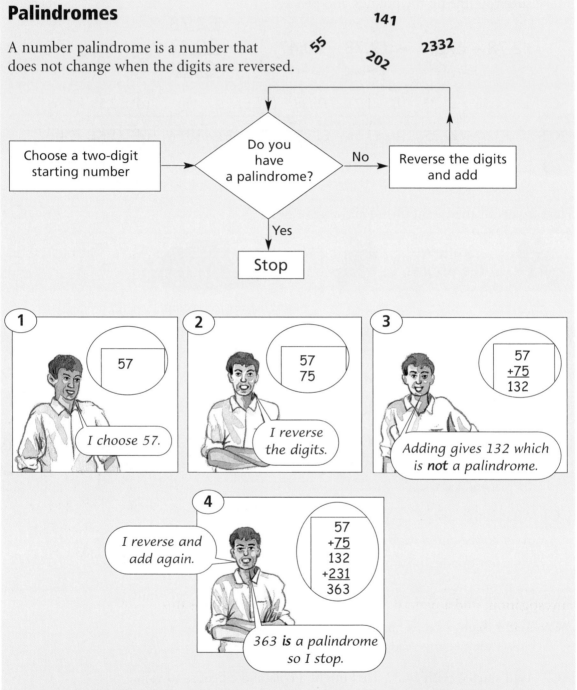

- Which numbers give a palindrome after one 'loop' round the flow diagram?
- How many loops do you need for other numbers?
- Do all numbers give palindromes in the end?

Number magic

Choose a two-digit number. The tens digit must be larger than the units.

Reverse the digits.

Subtract.

Reverse the result.

Add.

Example

$$
\begin{array}{r}
73 \\
-\ 37 \\
\hline
36 \\
+\ 63 \\
\hline
99 \\
\end{array}
$$

Repeat for some different starting numbers. What do you notice?

Extensions

• Repeat with three-digit numbers, then with four-digit numbers. The first digit must be larger than the last.

What progress have you made?

Statement	Evidence
I can do sums like 236 + 175 and 523 − 268 without a calculator.	1 Without using a calculator, work these out. (a) 341 + 516 (b) 373 + 48 (c) 479 + 153 (d) 649 − 135 (e) 342 − 26 (f) 523 − 346 (g) 410 − 69 (h) 314 − 137 (i) 605 − 179
I can add and subtract amounts of money without a calculator.	2 Without using a calculator, work these out. (a) £2.43 + £0.79 (b) £4.18 + 73p (c) £4.61 − £1.74 (d) £2.05 − 61p
I can carry out a number investigation, find a pattern and write about it.	Your work on 'Palindromes' and 'Number magic' shows this.

④ **Test it!**

This is about making and testing general statements about body measurements.
The work will help you

◆ measure accurately

◆ collect and record data

A I don't believe it!

Look at this statement.

'Everyone is
six and a half feet tall.'

Discuss these questions.

- *What does the statement mean?*
- *How could it be tested?*
- *What equipment will you need to test it?*

Draw up a plan together of how to test the statement.

Now put your plan into action.
Use it to answer the questions below.
(Don't be afraid to alter the plan as you go along.
Just make a note of any changes.)

- *Is the statement true for you?*
- *How true is it for your group?*
- *What about the rest of your class?*

B Organising your results

For class or group discussion

Amy, Ben, Emma and Anil have been set the task of testing this statement:

> People's heights are three times the distance round their heads.

They measure each other's height and head size.

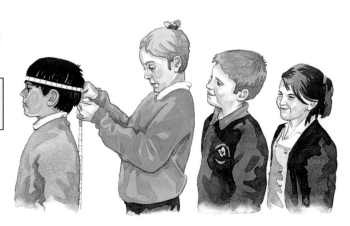

They write the measurements down.

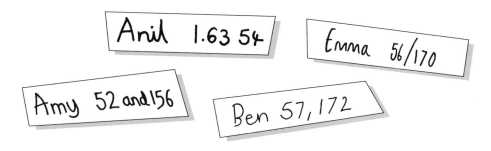

Anil 1.63 54

Emma 56/170

Amy 52 and 156

Ben 57, 172

B1 Look carefully at their measurements.
Can you make sense of them?
Would they mean anything to a stranger?
How would you improve their method of recording results?

Amy writes all their results in a table.

This helps them see any connections between height and head size.

Name	Head size (cm)	Height (cm)
Amy Allen	52	156
Anil Patel	54	163
Ben Arnot	57	172
Emma Pollock	56	170

B2 Ben says that their measurements show that

*'People's heights are approximately
three times the distance round their heads.'*

Is Ben's conclusion correct?

B3 A group of children measured themselves.
Here is their record of their data.

Name	Height (metres)	Distance round head (cm)	Arm span (cm)	Foot length (cm)	Head length (cm)	Hand span (cm)
Anna	1.41	53.5	152	19	21	16
Tim	1.63	57	1.70	29	23	20
Gina	14.4	54	143	21	21.5	19
Ajaz	1.49	55	153	22	23	19
Sue	159	59	157	2.6	23.5	21
Neena	1.48	54		23	23	19
Ryan	0.15	53	154	25	20.5	18
Lara	1.36	52	133	18	20.5	7
Majid	1.5	54	148	24	23.5	18

(a) What do you think 'head length' means?
    How would you measure it?

(b) Some children made mistakes.
    Find the mistakes and suggest what the measurements might be.

(c) To go on some fairground rides, you have to be at least 1.5 m tall.
    Who can go on these rides?

(d) Neena's arm span was not measured.
    Can you suggest what it might have been?

(e) In this group, whose height is closest to your height?
    Whose foot length is closest to your foot length?
    Whose arm span is closest to your arm span?

(f) Roughly how many times does head length go into height?

C Now it's your turn!

For two or more people

Here is a collection of statements about body size.

- The height of a person is equal to their arm span.
- People's waists are roughly twice the distance round their necks.
- A person's head length is half the distance across their shoulders.
- The distance round people's fists is the same as their foot length.

Choose one of the statements about body size.
Discuss how you would test it.
This checklist may help you.

- *How many people will we measure?*
- *What equipment will we need?*
- *How will we record the data?*
- *How can our group check the measuring and recording?*

Carry out your plan.
Do your results agree with the statement?

What progress have you made?

Statement

I can collect and record information.

I can test statements.

Evidence

Your work in sections A and C will show this.

1 Use the table below to check the statement: 'People are twice as high as their inside leg measurement.'

	Height (cm)	Inside leg (cm)
Peter	165	79
Annie	148	67
Amit	158	62
Tyler	172	83
Sonia	164	76
Carl	175	82

⑤ Reflection symmetry

This is about making shapes using mirrors and folding.
The work will help you

 ◆ make shapes that have reflection symmetry
 ◆ identify symmetrical shapes and their lines of symmetry

A Folding and cutting

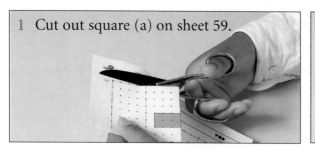

1 Cut out square (a) on sheet 59.

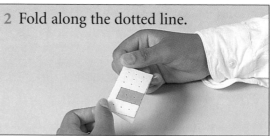

2 Fold along the dotted line.

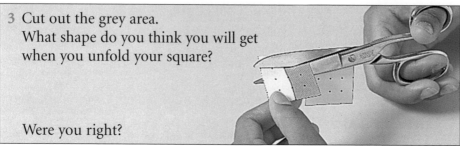

3 Cut out the grey area.
What shape do you think you will get
when you unfold your square?

Were you right?

A1 For each square (b) to (e) on sheet 59
 • draw the shape you think you will get if you
   fold along the dotted line and cut out the grey area
 • try it and see if you were right

A2 On square (f)
 • draw your own shape on one side of the dotted line
 • ask someone else to draw the shape you will get if
   you fold along the dotted line and cut out your shape
 • cut out the shape to see if they are right

A3 Draw the reflections of the shaded shapes on sheet 60.

A4 Draw the reflections of the shaded shapes on sheet 61.

*A5 Draw the reflections of the shaded shapes on sheet 62.

B Using a mirror

You need sheet 63.

B1 Put your mirror on the dotted line on diagram (a).

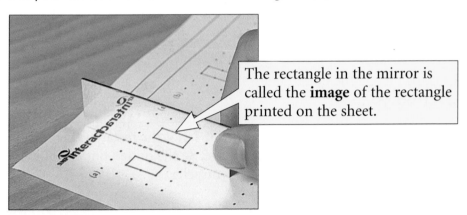

The rectangle in the mirror is called the **image** of the rectangle printed on the sheet.

Take the mirror away and
try to draw the image that you saw.

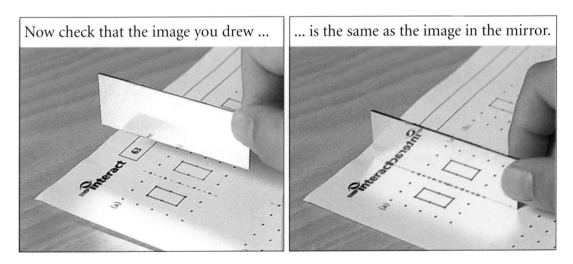

Now check that the image you drew ... ... is the same as the image in the mirror.

B2 Use a mirror to draw the images for diagrams (b) to (l).

After a while, you may be able to draw the image without using the mirror.
But always check with the mirror.

C Looking for reflection symmetry

Shapes you can make with a mirror or by folding and cutting are called **symmetrical**.

The fold or the place where the mirror goes is called a **line of symmetry**.

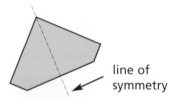

line of symmetry

C1
Put your mirror along the dotted line on shape (a) below.
The shape you see is symmetrical, but …

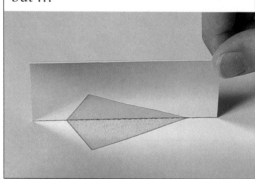

… it is not the rectangle printed on the page. So the dotted line is **not** a line of symmetry.

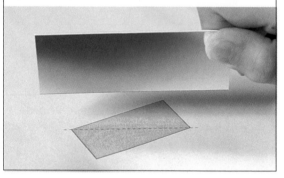

Is the dotted line a line of symmetry for each shape (b) to (h)?
Write 'yes' or 'no' for each one.
Check with your mirror.

(a)

(b)

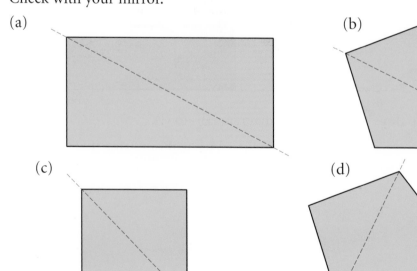

(c)

(d)

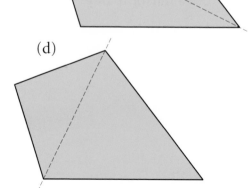

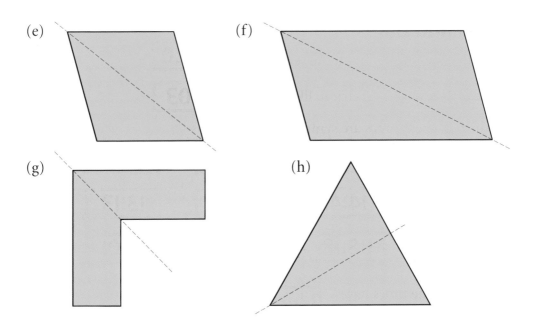

(e)

(f)

(g)

(h)

C2 Which of these designs are symmetrical?
Write 'yes' or 'no' for each one.
Check with your mirror.

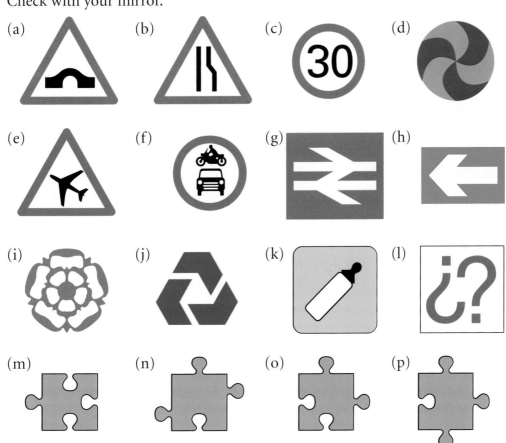

(a)

(b)

(c)

(d)

(e)

(f)

(g)

(h)

(i)

(j)

(k)

(l)

(m)

(n)

(o)

(p)

D Times and dates

Peter's computer shows the time on the screen. **06:20**

The times are sometimes symmetrical, like this: **18:03**

D1 (a) Which of these times are symmetrical?

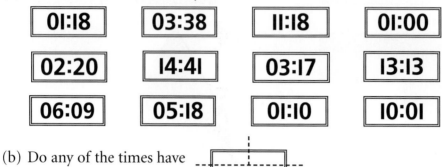

01:18	**03:38**	**11:18**	**01:00**
02:20	**14:41**	**03:17**	**13:13**
06:09	**05:18**	**01:10**	**10:01**

(b) Do any of the times have two lines of symmetry?

(c) Write three more times that have one line of symmetry.

(d) Write one more time that has two lines of symmetry.

Peter's computer shows the date in a similar way.

D2 11 November 2011 looks like this. **11:11:11**

How many lines of symmetry does it have?

D3 3 August 2001 looks like this. **03:08:01**

Is this date symmetrical?

D4 Say whether each of these dates has one, two or no lines of symmetry.

(a) **06:01:08**   (b) **18:11:81**

(c) **16:11:91**   (d) **08:10:13**

D5 Write these dates the way the computer shows them, and say how many lines of symmetry each one has.

(a) 4 February 2033   (b) 31 October 2081

(c) 8 November 2080   (d) 8 January 2080

D6 Write two more dates that have only one line of symmetry.

D7 Write two more dates that have two lines of symmetry.

Symmetry tiles game

for 2, 3 or 4 players

What you need

- You need a set of 25 tiles cut from sheet 64. There are five designs.

  Check that you have five tiles of each design.

- You also need a copy of board 1 on sheet 64.

The aim of the game

- You have to fill the board with a pattern that has a line of symmetry along the dotted line.

Before you start

- Make a score table like this with your own names.

Sue	Raf	Mary

- Deal out the tiles so each player has the same number. If there is a spare tile, don't use it.

When it is your turn

- Put one of your tiles on a square on the board. Remember that the pattern on the board must be symmetrical when the game is finished.

- Your score is the number you have covered up. Write your score in the score table.

- If you can't go you miss your turn.

End of game

- The game ends when all the squares on the board are covered or no player is able to go.

The winner

- The winner is the player with most points at the end of the game.

E Shading squares

E1 How many different ways can you shade
three squares in this design so that
it has reflection symmetry?
Sketch your different ways.

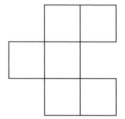

E2 Sketch all the different ways of shading
three squares in this design so that
it has reflection symmetry.

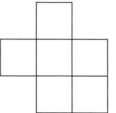

*E3 Sketch all the different ways of shading
three squares in this design so that
it has reflection symmetry.

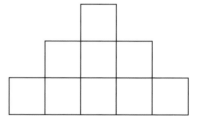

What progress have you made?

Statement

I can complete a symmetrical
shape when I have half of it.

I can draw a line of symmetry
on a symmetrical shape.

Evidence

1 Copy and complete these symmetrical
shapes.

(a)　　　　　　　　(b)

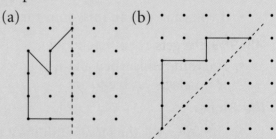

2 Copy this shape and draw
its line of symmetry.

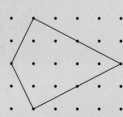

Multiplication tables

This work will help you learn the multiplication tables.

A Up to 5 × 5

Tables bingo

The caller has two dice, each numbered 0 to 5.
The dice are rolled to make multiplications.

Each player chooses seven numbers to
put on their 'bingo card'.

1	3	4	6	10	12	15

Rifle range

A1 Work out the score on each target.

(a) 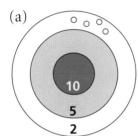   (b) 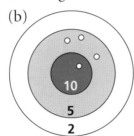   (c) 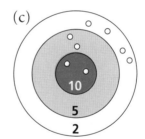   (d)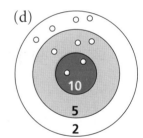

A2 These targets are different. Work out the score on each one.

(a) 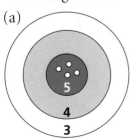   (b) 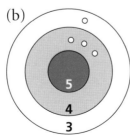   (c) 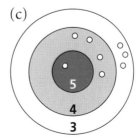   (d)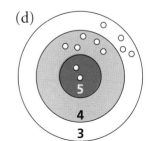

39

Roll-a-ball

A3 Work out the score in each of these games.

(a) (b) (c) (d)

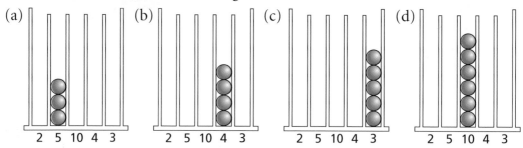

A4 Work out the score in each of these games.

(a) (b) (c) (d)

(e) (f) (g) (h)

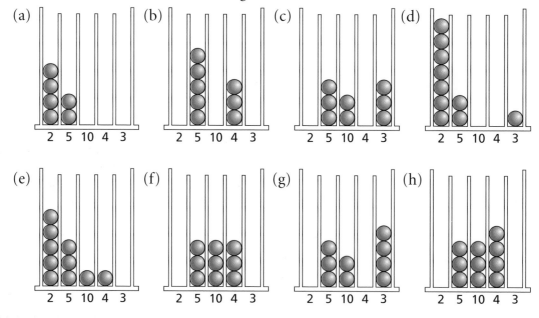

A5 Solve the roll-a-ball puzzles on sheet 28.

B Up to 10 × 10

How do you work out 6 × 8?

Jaspal

*I know that 5 × 8 = 40
so 6 × 8 = 40 + 8 = 48.*

Tina

*I know that 3 × 8 = 24
so 6 × 8 = 2 × 24 = 48.*

Diana

6 × 8 is the same as 8 lots of 6.

2 lots of 6 are 12.
Double to find 4 lots of 6 are 24.
Double again to find 8 lots of 6 are 48.

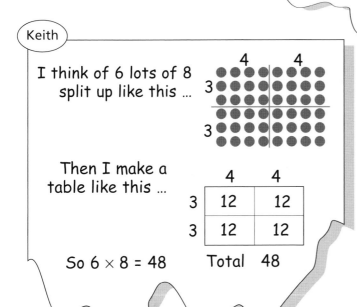

Keith

I think of 6 lots of 8
split up like this ...

Then I make a
table like this ...

	4	4
3	12	12
3	12	12

Total   48

So 6 × 8 = 48

*I just remember
that 6 × 8 = 48.*

Elaine

B1 Work these out as quickly as you can.

(a) 7×5 (b) 6×4 (c) 4×7

(d) 3×9 (e) 10×8 (f) 5×8

B2 Work these out as quickly as you can.

(a) 7×6 (b) 8×8 (c) 8×7

(d) 6×9 (e) 7×7 (f) 6×6

B3 Copy and complete this mixed-up multiplication table.

×	2	0	4
5	10	0	
3	6		
1			

B4 Copy and complete each mixed-up multiplication table.

(a)

×	5	2	4
3		6	
1			
0			

(b)

×	6	3	4
5			
3			12
2			

(c)

×	5	6	2
7			
10		60	
1			

(d)

×		4	7
8			
4			
5	10		

(e)

×	9	3	
8			
5			25
6			

(f)

×		7	6
9	81		
			48
7			

(g)

×	3	5	
	12		
1			
10			80

(h)

×	8		4
9			
	30	24	
7			

(i)

×			9
6			
	21	18	
4			

C Tables puzzles

C1 Copy and complete this mixed-up table.

	7	3	2	5
6	42	18	12	
4	28	12		
9				
8				

C2 In each table below, the numbers along the edges are 2, 3, 4, 5, 6, 7, 8 and 9.

They can be in any order, but each number is only used once.

Copy and complete each table.

(a)

	3	6	5	9
8				
			20	
7				

(b)

	8	5	9	
	21		15	
6				
2				

(c)

	9		7	
		18		6
		24		
5		30		

(d)

	3		4	
42		14		
			36	
	24			

(e)

	8	5		
	32		28	
9				
6	18			

(f)

	72	48	40	
			35	
12			15	

What progress have you made?

Statement	Evidence
I know the multiplication tables for 2, 3, 4 and 5.	**1** Do these in your head.

1 Do these in your head.

(a) 2 × 3   (b) 3 × 4   (c) 2 × 5

(d) 3 × 5   (e) 4 × 5   (f) 3 × 3

I know the multiplication tables up to 10.

2 Copy and complete these mixed-up multiplication tables.

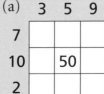

(a)

	3	5	9
7			
10		50	
2			

(b)

	7	8	
9			36
8			
		48	

 **Angle**

This work will help you

◆ understand acute, obtuse, reflex and right angles

◆ measure angles

◆ calculate angles on a straight line

A Making angles

Practical work is described in the teacher's guide.

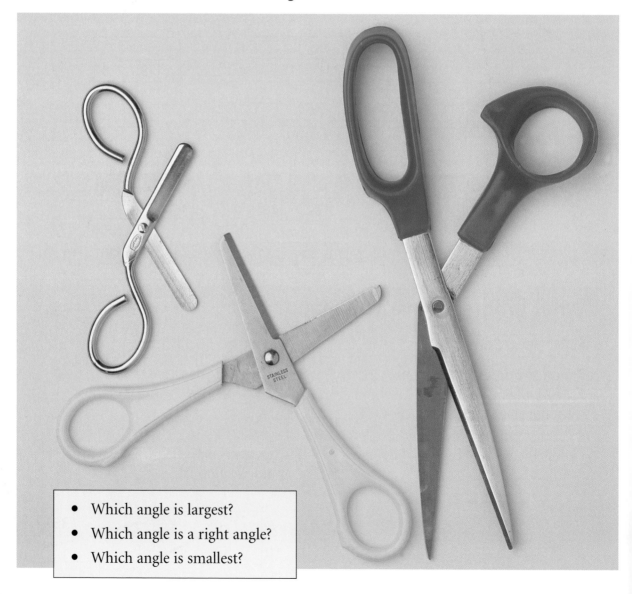

- Which angle is largest?
- Which angle is a right angle?
- Which angle is smallest?

B Comparing angles

You need tracing paper.

B1 Trace angle *X*.
Use your tracing to find which of the other angles are bigger than *X* and which are smaller.

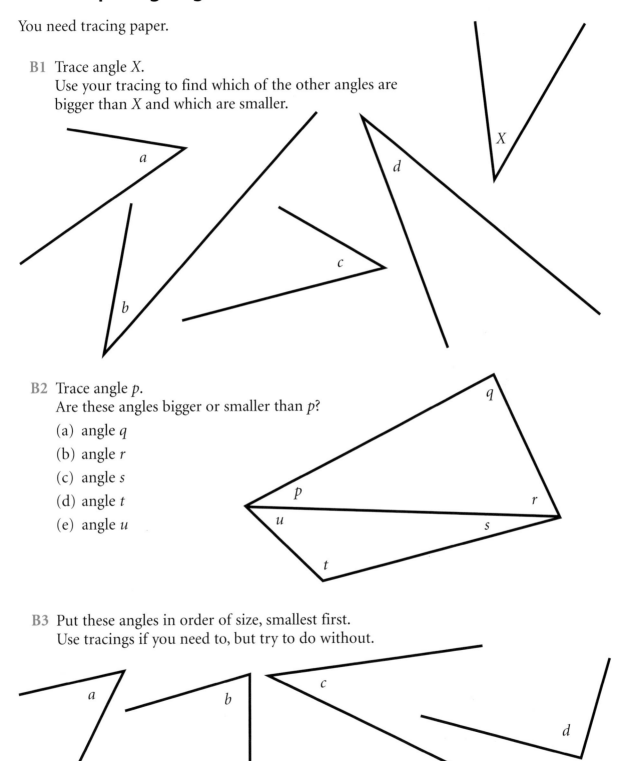

B2 Trace angle *p*.
Are these angles bigger or smaller than *p*?

  (a) angle *q*

  (b) angle *r*

  (c) angle *s*

  (d) angle *t*

  (e) angle *u*

B3 Put these angles in order of size, smallest first.
Use tracings if you need to, but try to do without.

C Right angles, acute, obtuse and reflex angles

An **angle** is made when a line turns from one position to another.

As the line turns, so the angle gets bigger … and bigger … and bigger …

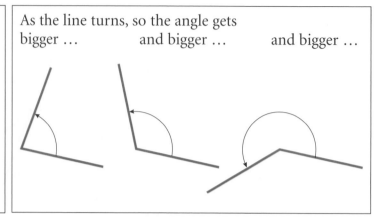

… until the line has made a **full turn**.

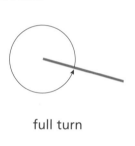

full turn

Each of these angles is a **half turn**.

half turn

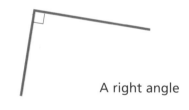

half turn

Each of these is a **quarter turn**.

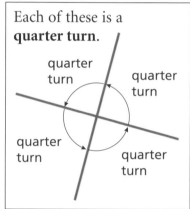

quarter turn   quarter turn

quarter turn   quarter turn

A quarter turn is also called a **right angle**.

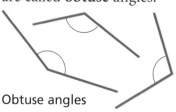

A right angle

The symbol for a right angle is a little square.

Angles that are smaller than a right angle are called **acute** angles.

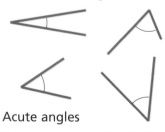

Acute angles

Angles that are bigger than a right angle (but less than two right angles) are called **obtuse** angles.

Obtuse angles

Angles that are bigger than two right angles are called **reflex** angles.

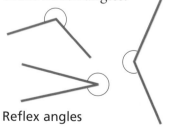

Reflex angles

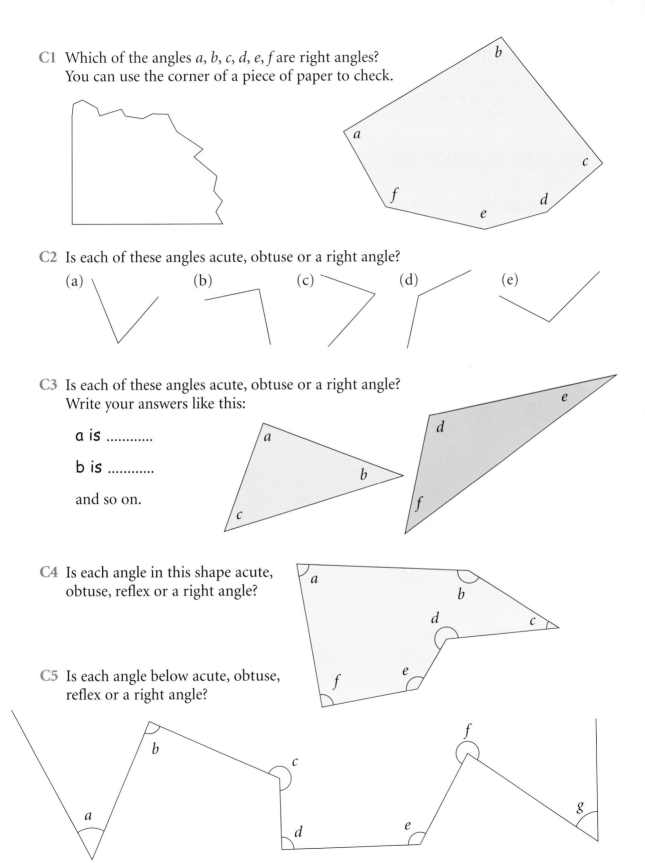

C1 Which of the angles *a*, *b*, *c*, *d*, *e*, *f* are right angles?
You can use the corner of a piece of paper to check.

C2 Is each of these angles acute, obtuse or a right angle?

(a) (b) (c) (d) (e)

C3 Is each of these angles acute, obtuse or a right angle?
Write your answers like this:

a is ....

b is ....

and so on.

C4 Is each angle in this shape acute,
obtuse, reflex or a right angle?

C5 Is each angle below acute, obtuse,
reflex or a right angle?

D Measuring angles

Angles are measured in **degrees**.
There are 360 degrees (**360°**) in a full turn.

How to use an angle measurer

Set the red pointer at 0.
Put the centre hole over the point of the angle.

Put the pointer along one arm of the angle.
Then move it round to the other arm.

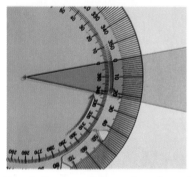

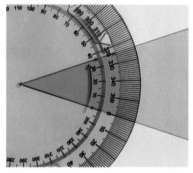

Read the outside scale when the
pointer goes clockwise.

Read the inside scale when the
pointer goes anti-clockwise.

D1 You need sheet 75, 76 or 77.

D2 Without measuring, say if there are any angles here
which look equal to each other.

Then check by measuring.

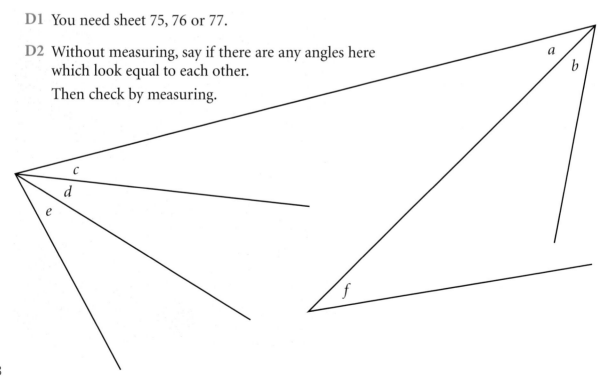

D3 (a) Measure the three angles of this triangle.

   (b) Add the three angles together.

   (c) Draw a triangle of your own and do the same.
       Do you get the same total?

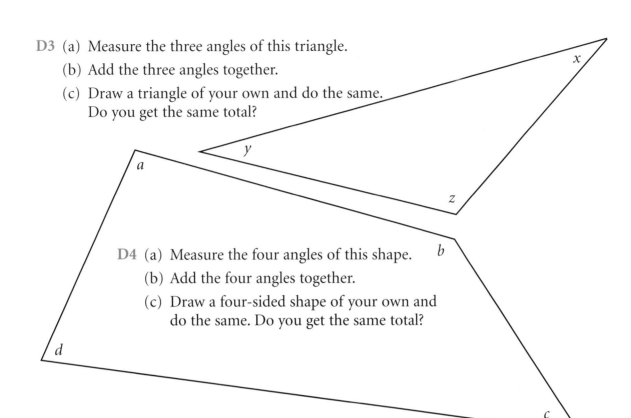

D4 (a) Measure the four angles of this shape.

   (b) Add the four angles together.

   (c) Draw a four-sided shape of your own and
       do the same. Do you get the same total?

Tilting bus

This bus is being tested to make sure it does not tip over easily.

What angle does the pointer on the front of the bus show?

What angle does the pointer on the side of the tilting platform show?

Why do you think they are different?

49

E Drawing angles

Using an angle measurer to draw an angle of 130°

1 Draw a line. Place the measurer so that the centre is on one end and the pointer covers the line. 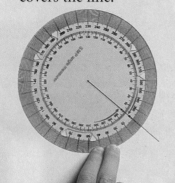	2 Turn the pointer to130°. Remember to use the correct scale. Make a mark at the end of the pointer. 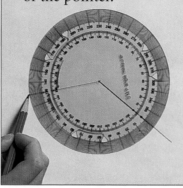	3 Draw the other arm of the angle through your mark. 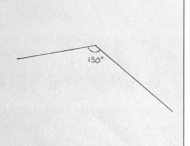 Label the angle with its size.

E1

Draw a line. Draw an angle of 50° at one end and an angle of 40° at the other, like this. 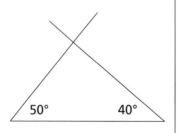	Measure the angle where these two lines meet. Write down its size. 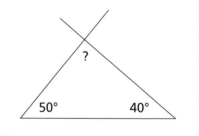

E2 Repeat E1 but with angles of 70° and 60°.

E3 Repeat E1 but with angles of 20° and 120°.

E4 Draw a four-sided shape with three of its angles 40°, 110° and 130°.

(a) Measure the fourth angle of the shape.

(b) Add all four angles together.

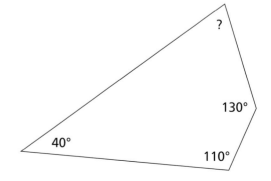

F Angles on a line

<table>
<tr>
<td>Draw an angle of 120°.
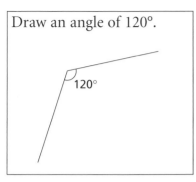</td>
<td>With a ruler extend one of the lines beyond the angle.
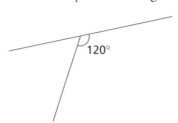</td>
<td>Measure the new angle you have made.
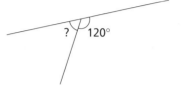

Add the two angles together.</td>
</tr>
</table>

Repeat this, starting with angles of

(a) 100°   (b) 70°   (c) 30°   (d) 90°

What do you notice?

F1 Calculate the angles marked with letters.

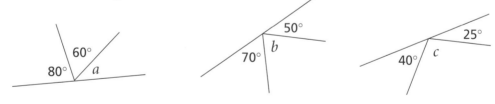

F2 Calculate the angles marked with letters.

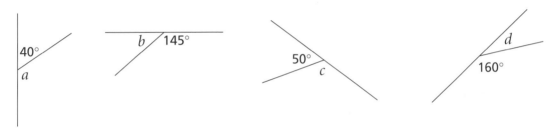

F3 Calculate the angles marked with letters.

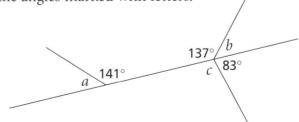

What progress have you made?

Statement

Evidence

I know what right angles, acute angles and obtuse angles are.

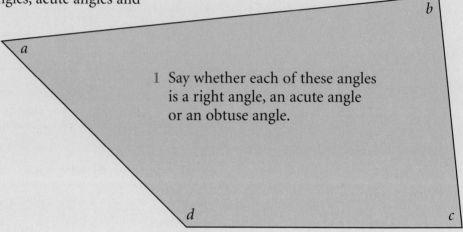

1 Say whether each of these angles is a right angle, an acute angle or an obtuse angle.

I can put angles in order of size.

2 Write the four angles above in order of size, smallest first.

I can measure angles.

3 Measure each angle above in degrees.

I can draw angles of a given size.

4 Draw a triangle with two of its angles 40° and 60°. Measure the third angle and write down its size.

I can use facts about angles on a line to calculate angles.

5 Calculate the angles marked with letters.

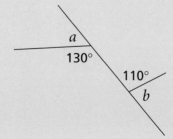

Oral questions: calendar

2011 calendar

January

Mon	Tue	Wed	Thu	Fri	Sat	Sun
					1	2
3	4	5	6	7	8	9
10	11	12	13	14	15	16
17	18	19	20	21	22	23
24	25	26	27	28	29	30
31						

February

Mon	Tue	Wed	Thu	Fri	Sat	Sun
	1	2	3	4	5	6
7	8	9	10	11	12	13
14	15	16	17	18	19	20
21	22	23	24	25	26	27
28						

March

Mon	Tue	Wed	Thu	Fri	Sat	Sun
	1	2	3	4	5	6
7	8	9	10	11	12	13
14	15	16	17	18	19	20
21	22	23	24	25	26	27
28	29	30	31			

April

Mon	Tue	Wed	Thu	Fri	Sat	Sun
				1	2	3
4	5	6	7	8	9	10
11	12	13	14	15	16	17
18	19	20	21	22	23	24
25	26	27	28	29	30	

May

Mon	Tue	Wed	Thu	Fri	Sat	Sun
						1
2	3	4	5	6	7	8
9	10	11	12	13	14	15
16	17	18	19	20	21	22
23	24	25	26	27	28	29
30	31					

June

Mon	Tue	Wed	Thu	Fri	Sat	Sun
		1	2	3	4	5
6	7	8	9	10	11	12
13	14	15	16	17	18	19
20	21	22	23	24	25	26
27	28	29	30			

July

Mon	Tue	Wed	Thu	Fri	Sat	Sun
				1	2	3
4	5	6	7	8	9	10
11	12	13	14	15	16	17
18	19	20	21	22	23	24
25	26	27	28	29	30	31

August

Mon	Tue	Wed	Thu	Fri	Sat	Sun
1	2	3	4	5	6	7
8	9	10	11	12	13	14
15	16	17	18	19	20	21
22	23	24	25	26	27	28
29	30	31				

September

Mon	Tue	Wed	Thu	Fri	Sat	Sun
			1	2	3	4
5	6	7	8	9	10	11
12	13	14	15	16	17	18
19	20	21	22	23	24	25
26	27	28	29	30		

October

Mon	Tue	Wed	Thu	Fri	Sat	Sun
					1	2
3	4	5	6	7	8	9
10	11	12	13	14	15	16
17	18	19	20	21	22	23
24	25	26	27	28	29	30
31						

November

Mon	Tue	Wed	Thu	Fri	Sat	Sun
	1	2	3	4	5	6
7	8	9	10	11	12	13
14	15	16	17	18	19	20
21	22	23	24	25	26	27
28	29	30				

December

Mon	Tue	Wed	Thu	Fri	Sat	Sun
			1	2	3	4
5	6	7	8	9	10	11
12	13	14	15	16	17	18
19	20	21	22	23	24	25
26	27	28	29	30	31	

⑨ Growing patterns

This is about investigating patterns.
The work will help you

◆ find patterns in a variety of situations

◆ describe how a pattern continues

◆ explain why a pattern continues in a particular way

A Coming up roses

This activity is described in the teacher's guide.

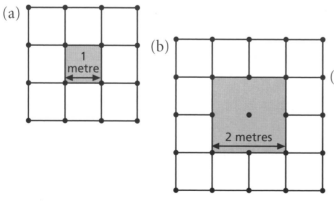

B Pond life

Joe works in a garden centre that sells square ponds
and square slabs to go round them.
Each slab measures 1 metre by 1 metre.

Joe works out how many slabs are needed for each pond.

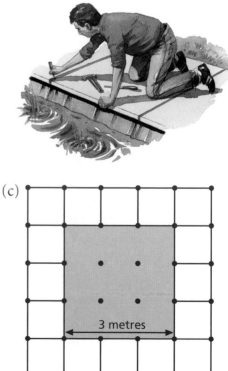

B1 Here are his diagrams for the first three ponds:

(a)

(b)

(c)

How many slabs are needed for each pond?

B2 (a) Draw a diagram for a pond that measures 4 by 4 metres.

(b) How many slabs are needed for this pond?

B3 (a) Draw a diagram for a pond that measures 5 by 5 metres.

(b) How many slabs are needed for this pond?

B4 (a) Copy and complete the table.

Side length of pond	1 metre	2 metres	3 metres	4 metres	5 metres	6 metres
Number of slabs						

(b) How many slabs do you think will be needed
for a pond that measures 7 by 7 metres?

(c) Check your result by drawing.

(d) How many slabs will be needed for a pond
that measures 10 by 10 metres?
Show how you worked this out.

B5 (a) What size of pond needs 48 slabs to go round it?
Show how you worked this out.

(b) What size pond needs 60 slabs?
Show your working.

B6 Joe makes a pond for Sima. The pond is 15 metres by 15 metres.
Joe needs 64 slabs.
Sima decides that instead she wants a 16 by 16 metre pond.

(a) How many **extra** slabs will Joe need?

(b) How many slabs are needed altogether for a 16 by 16 metre pond?

B7 (a) Describe how the number of slabs needed goes up
as the size of the pond goes up.

(b) Explain why the number of slabs goes up in this way.

B8 A 67 by 67 metre pond needs 272 slabs.
How many slabs are needed for a pond that measures 68 by 68 metres?

C Changing shape

C1 The garden centre also sells rectangular ponds.
All the rectangular ponds are 3 metres wide.

How many slabs are needed for these ponds?

(a)   (b)

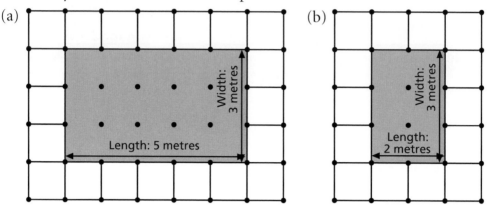

C2 (a) Draw a diagram for a 3 metre wide pond that is 6 metres long.

    (b) How many slabs are needed for this pond?

C3 (a) How many slabs do you think will be needed for
one of these ponds that is 7 metres long?

    (b) Check your answer by drawing.

C4 (a) Copy and complete this table for ponds like these.
Try to do it without any more drawing.

3 metre wide ponds							
Length of pond	1 metre	2 metres	3 metres	4 metres	5 metres	6 metres	7 metres
Number of slabs							

    (b) How many slabs do you think will be needed
for a 3 metre wide pond that is 8 metres long?
Show how you worked this out.

C5 (a) Describe how the number of slabs needed goes up as the size
of the pond goes up.

    (b) Explain why the number of slabs goes up in this way.

D Earrings

Chris is designing earrings with red and yellow beads.

How many different three-bead earrings can he make?

D1 How many different two-bead earrings can he make?

D2 Copy and complete the table.

Number of beads	1	2	3
Number of different earrings			

D3 (a) How many different four-bead earrings do you think can be made?

(b) Show how you found your answer.

(c) Check it by finding the different earrings.

D4 How many different five-bead earrings do you think can be made?

D5 Describe how the number of different earrings goes up with the number of beads.

What progress have you made?

Statement

I can find, use and explain patterns.

Evidence

Carol is planning a display of yellow and red rose bushes. Some designs for her display are shown below.

1 How many yellow rose bushes are needed for
  (a) 2 red rose bushes
  (b) 4 red rose bushes

2 Draw Carol's design for 3 red rose bushes.

3 Copy and complete this table for Carol's designs.

Number of red bushes	1	2	3	4	5
Number of yellow bushes					

4 (a) How many yellow bushes will be needed for 8 red bushes?
  (b) Show how you worked this out.

5 (a) How does the number of yellow bushes go up as the number of red bushes goes up?
  (b) Explain why the number of yellow bushes goes up in this way.

6 (a) How many yellow bushes will be needed for 10 red bushes?
  (b) Show how you worked this out.

⑩ Two-piece tangrams

① Rectangle

Start with a rectangle 7 cm by 4 cm.
Draw a diagonal.

You will need several copies.

Cut them out. Cut along the diagonal.

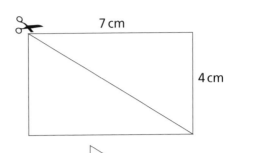

Put the two pieces together
by joining edges that have
the same length.

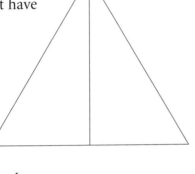

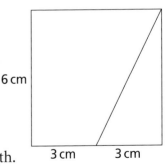

Not allowed!

Make all the possible shapes.
Record by sticking down or drawing.

*How do you know
you have got them all?*

② Square

Start with a square.

Join the midpoint of one side to an opposite corner.

You will need several copies.

Cut out and cut along the slanting line.

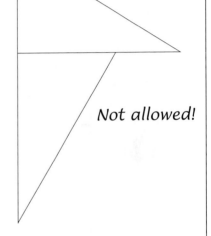

Put the pieces together. Join edges that are the same length.

Make all the possible shapes.
How do you know you have got them all?

11 Fractions

This work will help you

◆ understand halves, quarters, eighths and thirds
◆ write halves, quarters and eighths in order

A Fractions everywhere

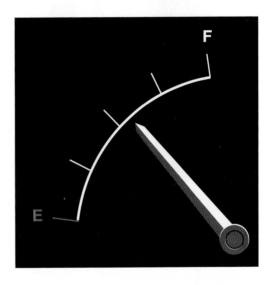

B Halves, quarters and what else?

Is a half coloured?

Is a quarter coloured?

If neither, can you say what fraction of the shape is coloured?

Explain your answers.

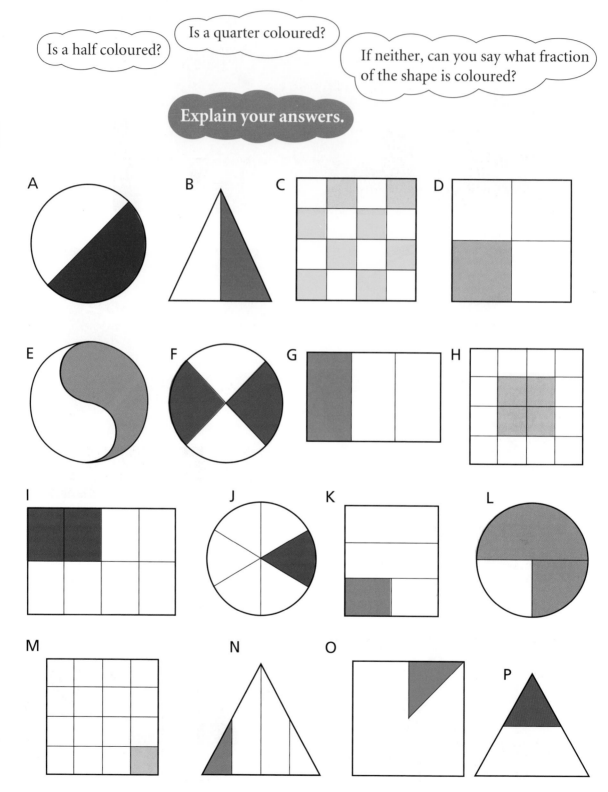

C Shade half, shade a quarter

You need sheet 36 or squared paper.

A half is written $\frac{1}{2}$.

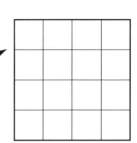

C1 Find different ways of shading $\frac{1}{2}$ of this square.
Here are some suggestions.

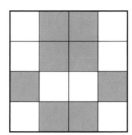 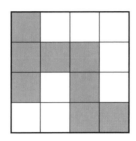

A quarter is written $\frac{1}{4}$.

C2 Find different ways of shading $\frac{1}{4}$ of the square.

D Thirds and what else?

The flag of Holland is divided into 3 **equal** parts.
Each part is **one third** of the flag.

One third is written $\frac{1}{3}$.

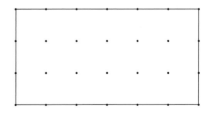

D1 Draw a rectangle this size on square dotty paper.
Shade $\frac{1}{3}$ of it.

Now draw some more rectangles the same size.
Shade $\frac{1}{3}$ of each one a different way.

D2 In which of these shapes is $\frac{1}{3}$ coloured?

A 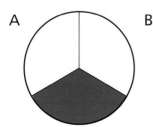 B 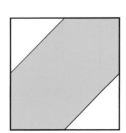 C 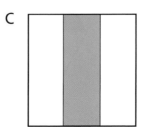 D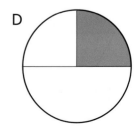

Two thirds of this square is coloured.

Two thirds is written $\frac{2}{3}$.

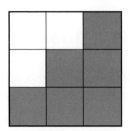

D3 Draw a square this size on square dotty paper.
Shade $\frac{2}{3}$ of it.

Now draw some more squares the same size.
Shade $\frac{2}{3}$ of each one a different way.

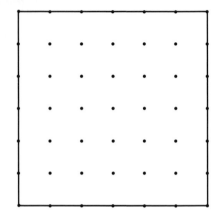

D4 In which of these shapes is $\frac{2}{3}$ coloured?

A 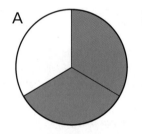   B 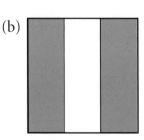   C 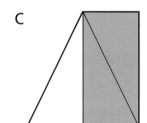   D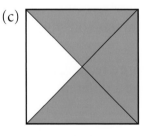

D5 What fraction is coloured in each of these, $\frac{1}{3}$, $\frac{2}{3}$ or something else?

(a) 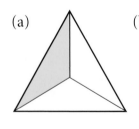   (b) 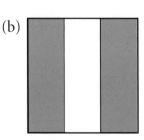   (c) 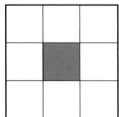   (d)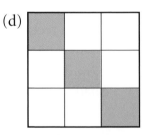

(e) 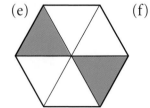   (f) 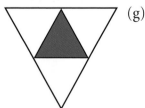   (g) 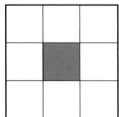   (h)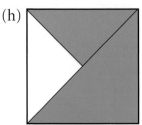

D6 Answer sections A, B and C on sheet 37.

E Eighths

This sheet of paper is divided into 8 equal parts.

Each part is $\frac{1}{8}$ of the sheet.

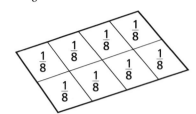

The green part is $\frac{1}{4}$ of the sheet.

It is the same as $\frac{2}{8}$ of the sheet.

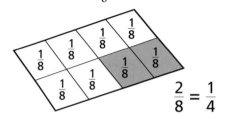

$$\frac{2}{8} = \frac{1}{4}$$

E1 Write each orange part as a fraction in at least two different ways.

(a)

(b)

(c)

(d)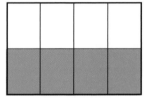

(e)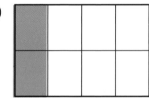

(f)

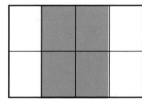

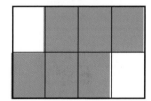

E2 (a) Make two copies of this rectangle on squared paper.

(b) On the first copy, shade $\frac{3}{4}$ of the rectangle.

(c) On the second copy, shade $\frac{7}{8}$ of the rectangle.

(d) Which is bigger, $\frac{3}{4}$ or $\frac{7}{8}$?

E3 In each of these pairs, which is the bigger fraction?

(a) $\frac{1}{4}$, $\frac{3}{8}$ (b) $\frac{5}{8}$, $\frac{1}{2}$ (c) $\frac{3}{4}$, $\frac{5}{8}$

E4 Write these fractions in order, smallest first.

$$\frac{1}{2} , \frac{5}{8} , \frac{1}{4} , \frac{3}{8}$$

What progress have you made?

Statement

I can identify halves, quarters and thirds.

Evidence

1 What fraction of each shape below is shaded?

(a)

(b)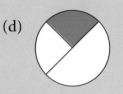

(c)

(d)

(e)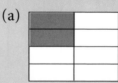

(f)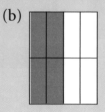

I can write some fractions in different ways.

2 Write each fraction in two different ways.

(a)

(b)

I can put some fractions in order.

3 Make two copies of this rectangle on squared paper.

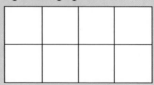

  (a) On one copy, shade $\frac{3}{8}$.

  (b) On the other copy, shade $\frac{3}{4}$.

  (c) Which is bigger, $\frac{3}{8}$ or $\frac{3}{4}$?

4 Write in order, smallest first.

$$\frac{7}{8}, \frac{1}{2}, \frac{3}{4}, \frac{1}{4}$$

Review 1

1 Copy these shapes and draw
their lines of symmetry.

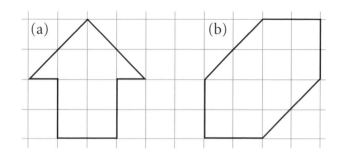

2 Which of the dotted lines are lines of symmetry?

(a)

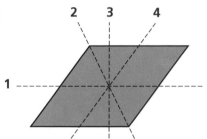

(b)

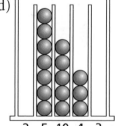

3 Work out the scores in each of these games.

(a)

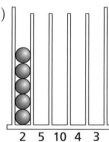

2 5 10 4 3

(b)

(c)

(d)

4 Copy and complete each mixed-up multiplication table.

(a)

	3	7	4	5
2		14		
3				
6				30
10				

(b)

	6	3		8
5			20	
6				
4				
		21		

(c)

	10	8		5
			42	
4				
3			18	
9				

5 Zoe is making displays of purple and yellow tulips.
Here are some of her displays.

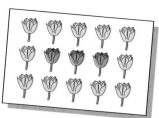

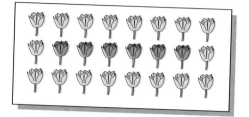 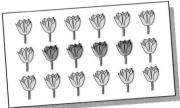

How many yellow tulips are needed for

(a) 5 purple tulips   (b) 1 purple tulip

6 Draw Zoe's display for 2 purple tulips.

7 Copy and complete this table for Zoe's displays.

Number of purple tulips	1	2	3	4	5	6
Number of yellow tulips						

8 (a) Without drawing, how many yellow tulips
would be needed for a display with 10 purples?

(b) One display needs 30 **yellow** tulips.
How many purple tulips are there?

9 (a) How does the number of yellow tulips go up
as the number of purples goes up?

(b) Explain why the number of yellow tulips goes up in this way.

10

a   *b*

(a) Say whether each of the angles inside this
shape is acute, obtuse or a right angle.

(b) Measure each of the angles in degrees.

d   *c*

11 (a) Draw a five-sided shape with four of its angles 80°, 165°, 90° and 120°.

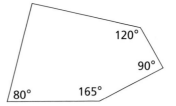

(b) Measure the fifth angle.

(c) Add all five angles together.

12 Calculate each angle marked with a letter.

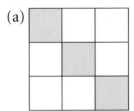
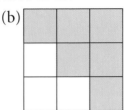
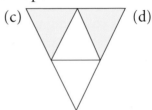

13 What fraction is coloured in each of these shapes?

(a) (b) (c) (d)

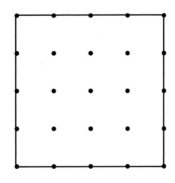

14 Make three copies of this square on square dotty paper.

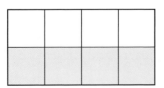

(a) Shade $\frac{1}{8}$ of the first square.

(b) Shade $\frac{5}{8}$ of the second square.

(c) Shade $\frac{3}{4}$ of the third square.

(d) Which is bigger, $\frac{5}{8}$ or $\frac{3}{4}$?

15 Copy and complete $\frac{4}{8} = \frac{}{4} = \frac{}{2}$.

16 Write these in order, smallest first.

$\frac{7}{8}, \quad \frac{1}{2}, \quad \frac{3}{4}, \quad \frac{5}{8}$

⑫ Coordinates

> This is about archaeological digs.
> The work will help you use coordinates.

A Recording positions

A farmer walked across his field one day.
He saw something shine in the ground.
He picked it up. It was a gold Roman coin
nearly 2000 years old.

The farmer wrote a letter to the local college.
He said a team of experts could dig up the field.

Dr Sanders came with a team of diggers.
She made careful notes every time a digger found
something.

She noted the exact place where each object was found.

The map opposite shows what the diggers found in the first month.
They found some walls and a few objects.

Look where the gold coins were found.

The **coordinates** of this point are **(1, 4)**.

metres **across** the field   metres **up** the field

A1 What was found at (a) (4, 1)   (b) (8, 5)   (c) (5, 8)

A2 Where did the diggers find these?

   (a) Broken pot

   (b) Bones

   (c) Bronze coins

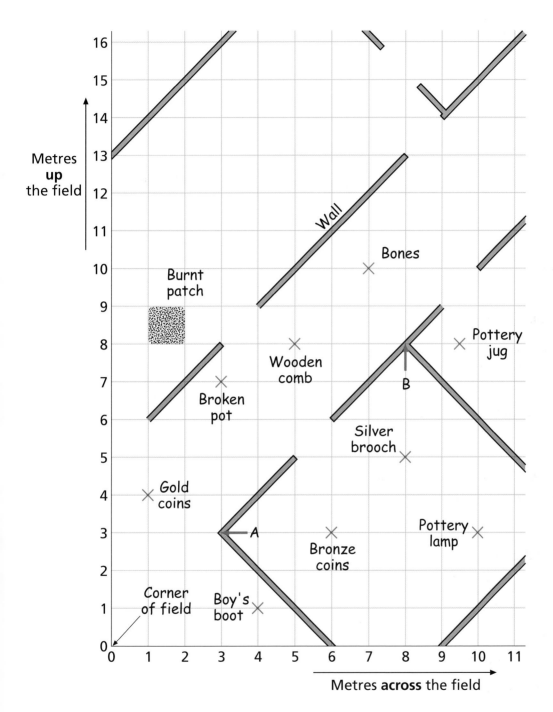

A3 What starts at (4, 9) and goes to (8, 13)?

A4 Find the corner of the field on the map. What are its coordinates?

A5 The corners of a room are labelled A and B.
What are their coordinates?

A6 You need sheet 67.

Here are Dr Sanders's notes for the second month.
Mark each object on the map and write its name.

Bones at (8, 14)

Broken pots at (2, 18) and (3, 15)

Grave between (2, 21) and (4, 20)

Arrowheads at (11, 15)

Wall from (5, 10) to (1, 14)

Parade helmet (8, 19)

Round grain pit 2 metres across
    centre at (4, 23)

Gold ring (15, 20)

Body scraper (13, 12)

Wall from (1, 6) to (0, 7)

Human skull (11, 23)

B Digging deeper

After one year the diggers decided to dig deeper.
They found the remains of buildings in layers.
The buildings got older as they dug deeper.

Level 1
(Last Roman)

Level 2
(Roman)

Level 3
(First Roman)

Level 4
(Iron Age)

There were four levels of old buildings.
Dr Sanders made a different map for each level.
The map you have used already is level 1.
The other levels are on sheets 68 and 69.

B1 You need sheet 68 (level 2).
Mark each of these objects on the map of level 2.

Level 2

Corn grinder (11, 18)

Silver cup (0, 6)

Glass bottle (5, 5)

Lady's shoe (3, 12)

Bones (7, 14)

Silver coins (7, 19)

Javelin head (8, 22)

Writing stylus (2, 1)

Bronze buckle (3, 18)

Comb (0, 9)

B2 You need sheet 69 (levels 3 and 4).
Mark each of these finds on the level 3 map.

> **Level 3**
>
> Gold bracelet $(1\frac{1}{2}, 14\frac{1}{2})$
>
>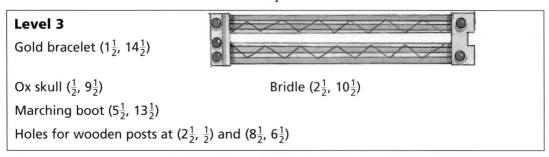
>
> Ox skull $(\frac{1}{2}, 9\frac{1}{2})$ Bridle $(2\frac{1}{2}, 10\frac{1}{2})$
>
> Marching boot $(5\frac{1}{2}, 13\frac{1}{2})$
>
> Holes for wooden posts at $(2\frac{1}{2}, \frac{1}{2})$ and $(8\frac{1}{2}, 6\frac{1}{2})$

B3 Mark each of these finds on the level 4 map.

> **Level 4**
>
>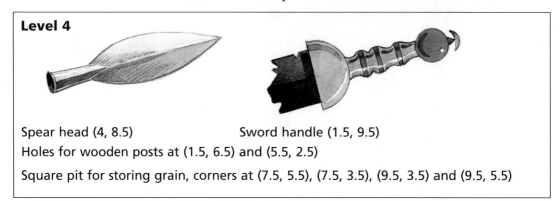
>
> Spear head $(4, 8.5)$ Sword handle $(1.5, 9.5)$
>
> Holes for wooden posts at $(1.5, 6.5)$ and $(5.5, 2.5)$
>
> Square pit for storing grain, corners at $(7.5, 5.5)$, $(7.5, 3.5)$, $(9.5, 3.5)$ and $(9.5, 5.5)$

What progress have you made?

Statement

I can write the coordinates of a point.

I can plot points on a grid.

Evidence

1 Write down the coordinates of A, B and C.

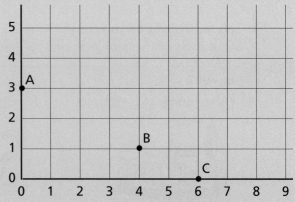

2 Copy the grid above and mark the points
D $(3, 4)$, E $(0, 2)$ and F $(1\frac{1}{2}, 4\frac{1}{2})$.

74

⑬ Area and perimeter

This work will help you

◆ work out the perimeter of a simple shape

◆ work out an area in square centimetres (cm²) or square metres (m²)

◆ work out a shape's area by splitting it into simpler shapes

A Exploring perimeters

Work on centimetre squared paper for these investigations.

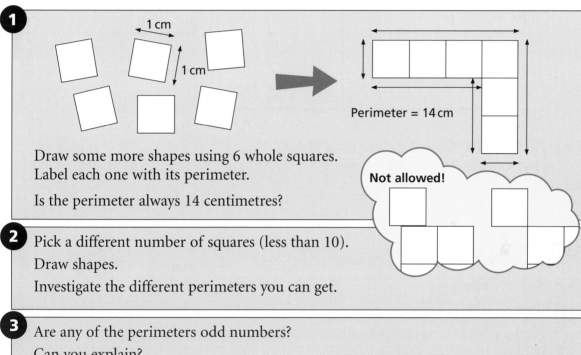

1

Draw some more shapes using 6 whole squares.
Label each one with its perimeter.

Is the perimeter always 14 centimetres?

Perimeter = 14 cm

Not allowed!

2 Pick a different number of squares (less than 10).
Draw shapes.
Investigate the different perimeters you can get.

3 Are any of the perimeters odd numbers?
Can you explain?

4 If you made shapes with 17 squares,
can you predict the largest perimeter you could get?
How do you work it out?
Explain why your method works.

5 Investigate the **smallest** perimeter you can get
for different numbers of squares.
Try to explain anything you find.

A1 These shapes are drawn on centimetre squared paper.
Find the perimeter of each shape.

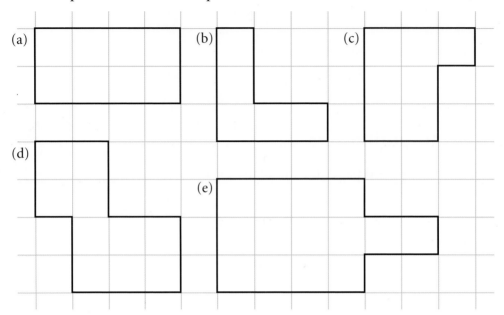

A2 Find the perimeter of each of these shapes.

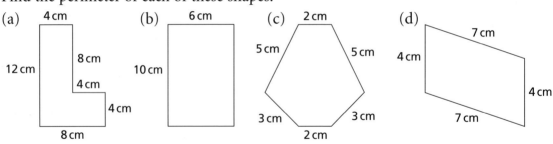

(a) 4 cm, 12 cm, 8 cm, 4 cm, 8 cm, 4 cm

(b) 6 cm, 10 cm

(c) 2 cm, 5 cm, 5 cm, 3 cm, 3 cm, 2 cm

(d) 7 cm, 4 cm, 7 cm, 4 cm

A3 These shapes are regular polygons.
All the sides of a regular polygon are the same length.

Find the perimeter of each shape.

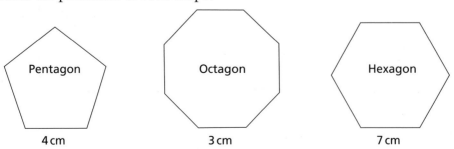

Pentagon 4 cm

Octagon 3 cm

Hexagon 7 cm

A4 A dodecagon has 12 sides.
What would the perimeter of a regular dodecagon be
if each side was 3 cm long?

B Square centimetres

The **area** of one square on this grid is **1 square centimetre.**

We write **1 cm²** for short.

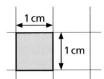

B1 What are the areas of these shapes?

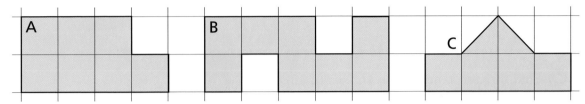

B2 (a) Which of these shapes has the largest area?

(b) Which has the smallest area?

(c) Do any of them have the same area?

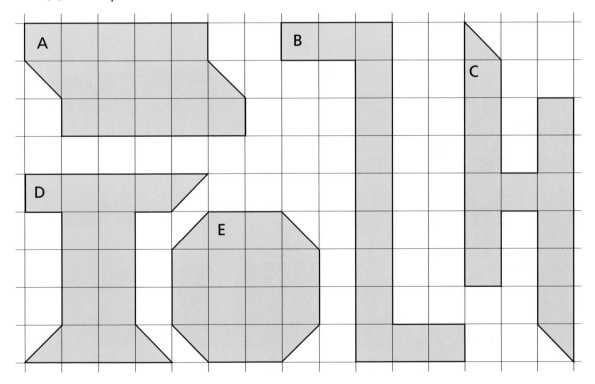

B3 On centimetre squared paper draw three shapes with areas that are nearly the same but not quite the same.

Give your shapes to a partner.
Challenge them to say which has the largest area just by looking.
Then they can check to see if they were right.

C The area of a rectangle

C1 What is the area of this rectangle in cm²?
Draw some other rectangles with the same area.

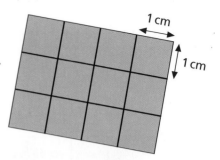

C2 Find three rectangles with an area of 40 cm².
Write down the length and width of each one.

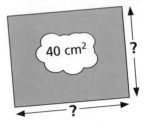

C3 How many rectangles can you find with an area of 16 cm²?
Write down the length and width of each one.

C4 Find the areas of these rectangles.

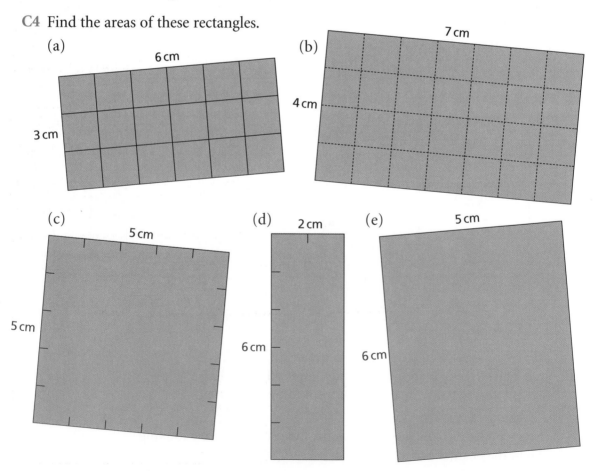

(a) 6 cm 3 cm

(b) 7 cm 4 cm

(c) 5 cm 5 cm

(d) 2 cm 6 cm

(e) 5 cm 6 cm

D Measuring to find areas

D1 A printer makes a set of gift tags.
Measure to find the area of each tag.

(a)

(b)

(c)

(d)

(e)

(f)

(g)

(h)

D2 (a) Just by looking, try to decide whether
more or less than half this rectangle
is shaded.

(b) Now measure and work out
whether you were right.

D3 Find the missing length for each rectangle.
(These are sketches, not accurate drawings.)

(a) Area = 14 cm² — 2 cm — ?

(b) Area = 35 cm² — 5 cm — ?

(c) Area = 32 cm² — ? — 8 cm

(d) Area = 48 cm² — 6 cm — ?

D4 Jon drew some rectangles.
Each rectangle had the same area.
His paper got torn.

How long were the missing sides?

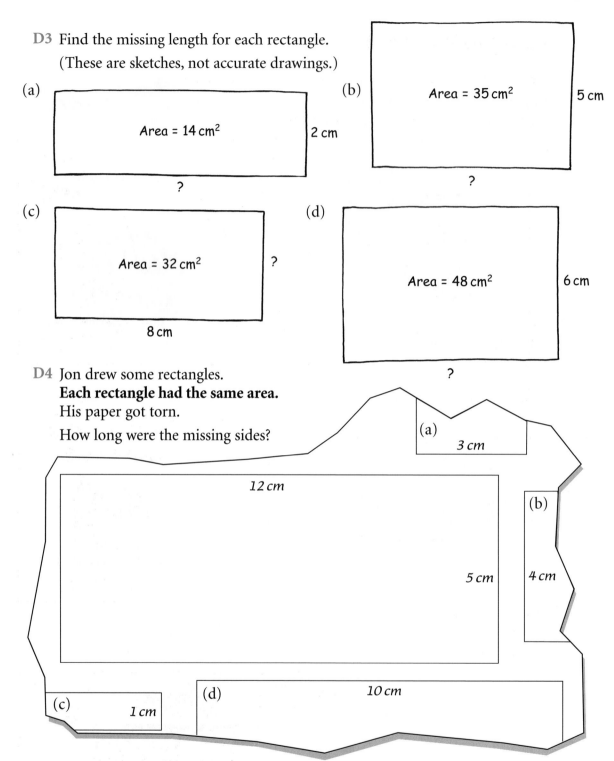

(a) 3 cm

12 cm

(b)

5 cm   4 cm

(c) 1 cm

(d) 10 cm

D5 The corners of a rectangle have these coordinates:
(0, 4), (9, 4), (9, 1), (0, 1)

Draw the rectangle on centimetre squared paper.
Find its area.

E It pays to advertise

E1 The Timesham *Weekly News* charges £1 per cm² for adverts.

How much will each of these cost?
(Write down your measurements each time.)

(a)

Fiona's Flowers

"They're blooming marvellous!!"

21 High St., Timesham

(b)

Summer Bonanza

Pine shelves £99
Bookshelves £89
Pine beds £199
Tables £129

THE PINE PLACE

(c)

Mary's Cattery

The "Purrfect" home from home for your cat
Tel: Timesham 987654

(d)

Chequers
Night Club

Why not check us out!

Fridays, The Brewhouse
Old Market St. 11 – 3am

(e)

R G SPARK & SON

ELECTRICAL CONTRACTORS & ENGINEERS

___

COMMERCIAL•INDUSTRIAL
• RETAIL

Installers of:
- Lighting
- Alarms
- Cabling
- Inspection & Testing

___

Unit 4, Timesham Business Park   Tel: 123467

(f)

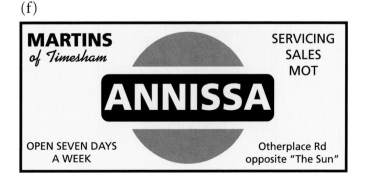

MARTINS
of Timesham

ANNISSA

SERVICING
SALES
MOT

OPEN SEVEN DAYS
A WEEK

Otherplace Rd
opposite "The Sun"

E2 The Timesham *Evening Echo* has more readers.
So it can charge £2 per cm² for adverts.

How much will each of these cost?
(Write down your measurements.)

(a)

GARDEN SUPPLIES

Specialists in Garden Furniture
Many styles of Tables and chairs,
Pergolas, Fencing etc.

Timesham 123578

(b)

B. F. Pie

Quality
Butcher

Prizewinning game sausages

Free Local delivery

14 Lamb St., Lower Timesham
Telephone: 876543

(c)

THE SUN INN   Tel: 124689

Fine Pub Food
A selection of Real Ales
Traditional games
A la carte restaurant and function room

(d)

Plumbing problem?
Call Lee King
for emergency service
24 hrs Mobile 0808 888222

(e)
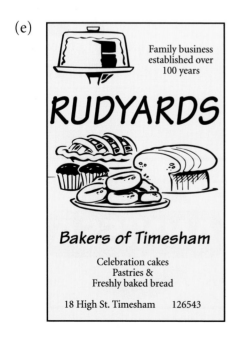

Family business
established over
100 years

RUDYARDS

Bakers of Timesham

Celebration cakes
Pastries &
Freshly baked bread

18 High St. Timesham   126543

(f)

Diana's
Mobile hairdressing

TELEPHONE: 777 242424

✂ D. Salon MPHA

F Square metres

The areas of floors, walls, gardens and so on are measured in square metres (m² for short). Square centimetres are too small.

Estimate these in square metres:

- the area of your classroom floor
- the area of one of the walls

Now measure to see how close you were.

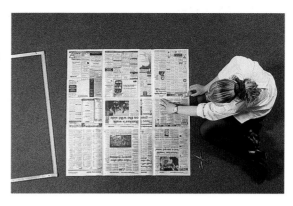

F1 Find the area of the whole of this floor in square metres.

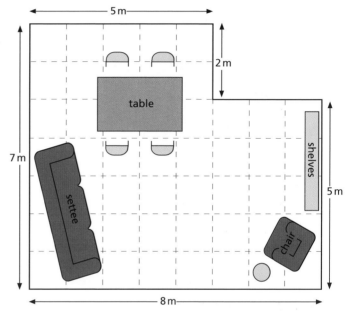

You can find the area of some 'awkward' shapes by splitting them into rectangles.

For example, this L-shape can be split into two rectangles A and B.

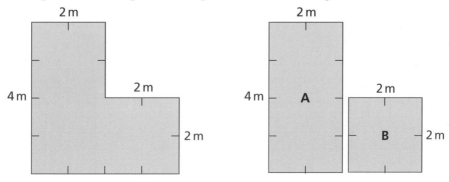

F2 (a) What is the area of rectangle A?

(b) What is the area of rectangle B?

(c) What is the area of the whole L-shape?

F3 Draw a sketch of this L-shape.
Split it into rectangles.
Work out the area of the whole shape.

Now split it a different way to
work out the area of the whole shape.

Check that both ways give you the same area.

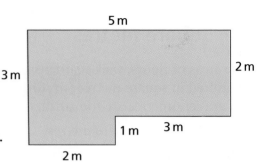

F4 **Work with a partner.**
Work out the area of each of the shapes below.
You split up each shape one way, and your partner splits them in another way.

Check you both get the same answers.

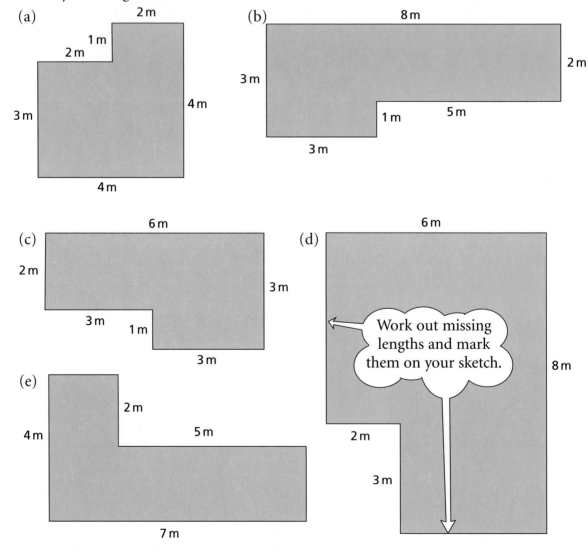

F5 Work out the perimeters of the shapes in question F4.

Safely grazing

An investigation

A shepherdess wants to make a pen for her sheep.
She only has 40 m of fencing.

This is one possible pen
she could make.

What is the area of this pen?

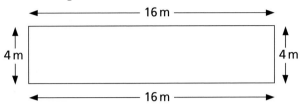

Draw some other rectangular pens she could make using all her fencing.
Find the areas of these pens.

What length and width give the biggest area of pen?

Try with some other lengths of fencing.
Draw some sketches and write about your findings.

What progress have you made?

Statement

I can find the area and perimeter of
a rectangle.

Evidence

1 Measure this label.
Work out its area and perimeter.

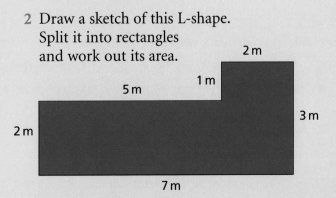

I can find areas and perimeters of
shapes by splitting them up.

2 Draw a sketch of this L-shape.
Split it into rectangles
and work out its area.

85

⑭ Rounding

This work will help you

- ◆ know what each digit in a number means
- ◆ recognise values on a number line
- ◆ round numbers to the nearest ten, hundred or thousand

A Place value

Place value bingo

The cards for this game are made from sheet 26.

| 2002 | 2030 | 2033 | 2300 | 3002 |
| 3003 | 3020 | 3200 | 3302 | 3322 |

Three thousand and twenty

Can I cover up any of my numbers?

A1 In the number **2639**, the figure **3** means **3 tens** or **30**.
What do these digits mean?

(a) the 5 in 2593   (b) the 7 in 7831   (c) the 8 in 4086

(d) the 8 in 7841   (e) the 6 in 1362   (f) the 9 in 9428

A2 What do you get if you

(a) add 10 to 4573   (b) add 100 to 4573   (c) add 1000 to 4573

(d) add 100 to 6097   (e) add 1000 to 6097   (f) add 10 to 6097

A3 In your head, work out what number is

(a) 1 less than 400   (b) 1 less than 7000   (c) 10 less than 7100

(d) 100 less than 7000   (e) 10 less than 2000   (f) 100 less than 3000

A4 In your head, work out what number is

(a) 10 more than 3472   (b) 100 more than 5623   (c) 10 less than 2395

(d) 1000 less than 2304   (e) 100 less than 4278   (f) 100 less than 5162

(g) 10 less than 8400   (h) 100 more than 4900   (i) 10 more than 3992

B Number lines

B1 (a) What does each small space on this number line stand for?

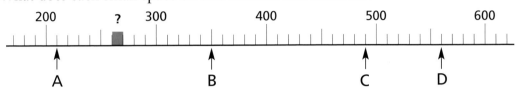

(b) What number does each arrow point to?

B2 (a) What does each small space on this number line stand for?

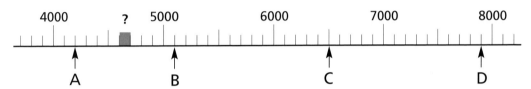

(b) What number does each arrow point to?

B3 Answer the questions on sheet 27.

C Nearest ten

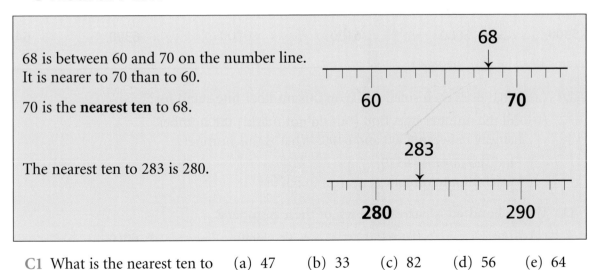

68 is between 60 and 70 on the number line.
It is nearer to 70 than to 60.

70 is the **nearest ten** to 68.

The nearest ten to 283 is 280.

C1 What is the nearest ten to   (a) 47   (b) 33   (c) 82   (d) 56   (e) 64

C2 What is the nearest ten to   (a) 141   (b) 269   (c) 438   (d) 862   (e) 708

C3 What is the nearest ten to   (a) 99   (b) 503   (c) 296   (d) 106   (e) 394

75 is exactly halfway between 70 and 80.
So there are two 'nearest tens' to 75.
But we usually go **up** and call 80 the 'nearest'
ten to 75.

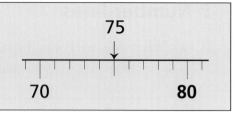

C4 What is the 'nearest' ten to (a) 65 (b) 35 (c) 85 (d) 95 (e) 15

C5 What is the 'nearest' ten to (a) 175 (b) 285 (c) 495 (d) 605 (e) 355

C6 Use this number line to help you find the nearest ten to
(a) 1376 (b) 1388 (c) 1397 (d) 1404 (e) 1405

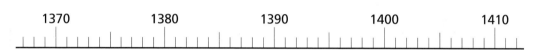

C7 What is the nearest ten to each of these numbers?
(a) 4623 (b) 6385 (c) 5002 (d) 2183 (e) 3868
(f) 2196 (g) 3005 (h) 4739 (i) 2449 (j) 1996

D Nearest hundred, nearest thousand

D1 (a) What does each small space on this number line stand for?
(b) On the number line, find (but do not mark!) the number halfway between 6300 and 6400. What is this number?
(c) Find the number 6370.
Which hundred mark is nearest to 6370?

D2 Which hundred is nearest to each of these numbers?
(a) 6120 (b) 6280 (c) 5930 (d) 6010
(e) 5980 (f) 6170 (g) 6420 (h) 6460

6250 is halfway between 6200 and 6300.
We go **up** and say that **6300** is the 'nearest'
hundred to 6250.

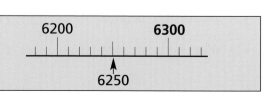

D3 What is the 'nearest' hundred to each of these?

    (a) 6350   (b) 6150   (c) 6050   (d) 5950

D4 Find roughly (without marking) where 6163 is on the number line on page 88. What is the nearest hundred to 6163?

D5 What is the nearest hundred to each of these?

    (a) 6384   (b) 5937   (c) 6065   (d) 5971

    (e) 6209   (f) 6416   (g) 6152   (h) 5948

Finding the nearest hundred to a number is called
rounding to the nearest hundred.

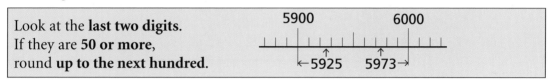

Look at the **last two digits.**
If they are **50 or more,**
round **up to the next hundred.**

We round a number when we only need to know it roughly.

D6 Round these numbers to the nearest hundred.

    (a) 4138   (b) 7876   (c) 2465   (d) 5093

    (e) 2047   (f) 5184   (g) 6961   (h) 4752

    (i) 3506   (j) 3009   (k) 6385   (l) 9772

You can also round larger numbers to the nearest thousand.

15 000   16 000   17 000   18 000   19 000   20 000

D7 (a) What does each small space on this number line stand for?

    (b) On the number line, find the number halfway between 17 000 and 18 000. What is this number?

    (c) On the line, find 17 800. Which thousand is 17 800 nearest to?

D8 Which is the nearest thousand to

    (a) 17 400   (b) 17 900   (c) 17 260

D9 Round these numbers to the nearest thousand.

    (a) 16 200   (b) 16 750   (c) 15 180   (d) 15 920

    (e) 19 150   (f) 18 020   (g) 18 634   (h) 15 490

    (i) 18 973   (j) 17 099   (k) 15 854   (l) 19 955

What progress have you made?

Statement

I know what each digit means in a number.

I can read number lines.

Evidence

1 (a) What does the 6 in 3067 mean?

(b) What number is 100 less than 4195?

2 What numbers do the arrows point to?

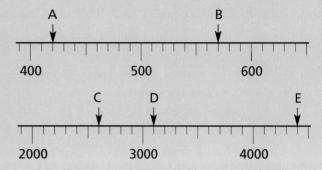

I can round numbers to the nearest ten.

3 What is the nearest ten to each of these numbers?

(a) 43 (b) 57 (c) 61 (d) 98

4 What is the nearest ten to each of these numbers?

(a) 483 (b) 567 (c) 2478 (d) 2697

I can round numbers to the nearest hundred.

5 Round each of these numbers to the nearest hundred.

(a) 6330 (b) 6490 (c) 5880 (d) 4130

6 Round each of these numbers to the nearest hundred.

(a) 6865 (b) 2059 (c) 1972 (d) 5144

I can round numbers to the nearest thousand.

7 Round each of these to the nearest thousand.

(a) 15 400 (b) 17 100 (c) 18 900

8 Round these to the nearest thousand.

(a) 17 500 (b) 23 250 (c) 39 875

Mostly multiplication

This work will help you
◆ understand multiplication and division by 10, 100 and 1000
◆ multiply whole numbers without using a calculator

A Multiplying by 10, 100 and 1000

Our way of writing numbers is called a **place value** system.
The place of a digit tells you what its value is.

When you multiply by 10,

- a unit becomes a ten
- a ten becomes a hundred
- a hundred becomes a thousand

The picture shows what happens
when you multiply 647 by 10.

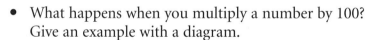

Each digit moves one place to the left.
A zero is put in the units place.

- What happens when you multiply a number by 100?
  Give an example with a diagram.

- What happens when you multiply by 1000?

A1 Write down the results of these multiplications.
  (a) 26×10 (b) 26×100 (c) 48×100 (d) 324×100 (e) 66×100

A2 Write down the results of these.
  (a) 30×10 (b) 40×100 (c) 601×10 (d) 300×100 (e) 806×100

A3 Write down the results of these.
  (a) 100×30 (b) 420×10 (c) 100×269 (d) 300×10 (e) 100×45

A4 Write down the results of these.
  (a) 6×1000 (b) 36×100 (c) 84×1000 (d) 24×100 (e) 66×1000

A5 Write down the results of these.
  (a) 1000×30 (b) 650×100 (c) 1000×55 (d) 100×100 (e) 1000×54

A6 Copy and complete these multiplications.

(a) $15 \times ? = 150$ (b) $27 \times ? = 2700$ (c) $? \times 34 = 34\,000$ (d) $100 \times ? = 2400$

A7 (a) Multiply four hundred and six by ten.
Write the result in figures and then in words.

(b) Multiply two thousand and fifty by ten.
Write the result in words.

(c) Multiply six hundred and five by a hundred.
Write the result in words.

B Metric units

There are 10 millimetres in 1 centimetre.
$4\,cm = 4 \times 10\,mm = 40\,mm$.

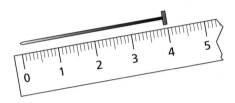

There are 100 cm in 1 metre.
$3\,m = 3 \times 100\,cm = 300\,cm$.

B1 Change these lengths in centimetres to millimetres.

(a) 6 cm   (b) 2 cm   (c) 15 cm   (d) 25 cm   (e) 50 cm

(f) 130 cm   (g) 175 cm   (h) 283 cm   (i) 500 cm   (j) 1200 cm

B2 An engineer has a steel rod 30 cm long.
How long, in millimetres, would the rod be if she cuts off these lengths?

(a) 7 mm   (b) 12 mm   (c) 23 mm

B3 Change these lengths in metres to centimetres.

(a) 8 m   (b) 12 m   (c) 25 m   (d) 50 m   (e) 100 m

(f) 240 m   (g) 145 m   (h) 375 m   (i) 800 m   (j) 1500 m

B4 Sanjay has a piece of material 5 m long.
How much material would he have left, in centimetres,
if he cut these lengths from the piece?

(a) 30 cm   (b) 150 cm   (c) 2 m 70 cm

B5 There are a thousand grams in one kilogram.
Change these measurements in kilograms to grams.

(a) 5 kg   (b) 15 kg   (c) 50 kg   (d) 200 kg   (e) 125 kg

B6 Russell has a 2 kg bag of flour.
How much flour, in grams, would he have left if he used these amounts?

(a) 500 g   (b) 250 g   (c) 1200 g

C Dividing by 10, 100, …

When you divide by 10,

a ten becomes a unit,

a hundred becomes a ten,

a thousand becomes a hundred.

The picture shows what happens
when you divide 6470 by 10.

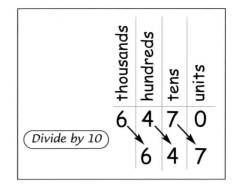

- What happens when you divide a number by 100?
  Give an example with a diagram.

- What happens when you divide by 1000?

C1 Work these out.

(a) 450 ÷ 10　　　(b) 3200 ÷ 10　　　(c) 457 000 ÷ 100　(d) 1300 ÷ 100

(e) 36 000 ÷ 10　　(f) 83 000 ÷ 100　　(g) 80 000 ÷ 10　　(h) 10 200 ÷ 100

(i) 20 000 ÷ 100　(j) 59 000 ÷ 1000　(k) 3000 ÷ 10　　　(l) 13 000 ÷ 10

C2 Here is a list of numbers.

600	45	3000	6	30	450	78 000
78	60	3	60 000	45 000	780	

How many ways can you find to complete each division below,
using only numbers in the list above?

(a) ☐ ÷ 10 = ☐

(b) ☐ ÷ 100 = ☐

(c) ☐ ÷ 1000 = ☐

C3 Work these out.

(a) 190 ÷ 10　　(b) 190 × 10　　(c) 362 000 ÷ 100　　(d) 362 000 × 100

C4 Change these lengths in millimetres to centimetres.

(a) 290 mm　(b) 3700 mm　(c) 500 mm　(d) 8000 mm　(e) 7500 mm

C5 Change these lengths in centimetres to metres.

(a) 3500 cm　(b) 25 000 cm　(c) 3000 cm　(d) 300 cm　(e) 1000 cm

D The 20, 30, ... times tables

- Do you need to learn the 20 times table?
  The 30 times table?
- Do you need to learn the 200 times table?
  If not, why not?

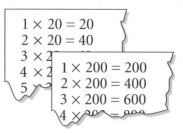

$1 \times 20 = 20$
$2 \times 20 = 40$
3×2
4×2 $1 \times 200 = 200$
5 $2 \times 200 = 400$
  $3 \times 200 = 600$
$4 \times$

D1 Write down the results of these multiplications.

(a) 4×20 (b) 20×6 (c) 8×20 (d) 30×5 (e) 3×30

(f) 40×3 (g) 4×50 (h) 60×3 (i) 6×50 (j) 40×2

D2 Write down the results of these.

(a) 200×3 (b) 4×300 (c) 500×2 (d) 300×5 (e) 600×4

(f) 4×500 (g) 600×3 (h) 3×500 (i) 800×2 (j) 3×700

D3 Susan says that 40×30 is 120.
How would you convince her that she is wrong?

D4 Work these out.

(a) 20×30 (b) 20×50 (c) 80×20 (d) 60×30 (e) 40×50

D5 Work these out.

(a) 300×20 (b) 40×300 (c) 50×60 (d) 20×700 (e) 400×50

(f) 300×200 (g) 600×50 (h) 70×30 (i) 400×80 (j) 50×50

D6 Work these out.

(a) 30×30 (b) 40×40 (c) 50×50 (d) 80×80 (e) 200×200

In the list

Look at the numbers in this list.

You can make multiplications using
only numbers in the list.

For example, $20 \times 40 = 800$

You can use the same number twice.

For example, $20 \times 20 = 400$

The result has to be in the list.
So you **cannot** have $80 \times 800 = 64\,000$,
because $64\,000$ is not in the list.

| 20 |
| 40 |
| 80 |
| 160 |
| 400 |
| 800 |
| 1600 |
| 3200 |
| 8000 |

What multiplications can you make using only numbers in the list?

E Area and multiplication

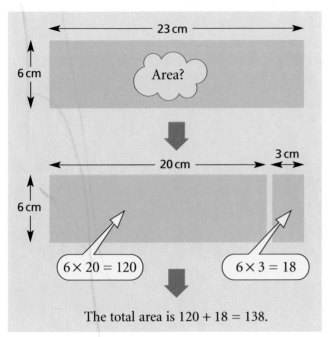

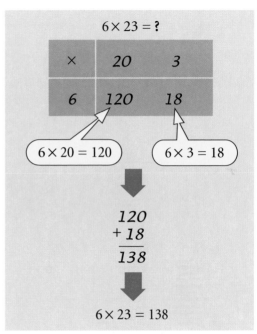

The total area is 120 + 18 = 138.

$6 \times 23 = 138$

E1 This large rectangle has been split into two smaller rectangles.

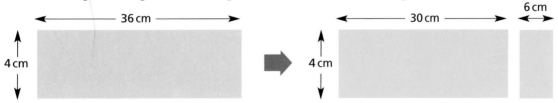

(a) Find the area of the two smaller rectangles.

(b) Write down the area of the large rectangle.

E2 Work out the area of these rectangles by splitting them into two smaller ones.

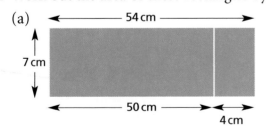

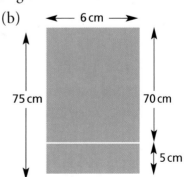

E3 Find the areas of these rectangles by splitting each one into smaller rectangles. Make rough sketches to show how you split each one.

(a)

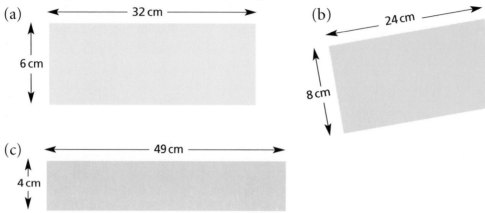

32 cm

6 cm

(b)

24 cm

8 cm

(c)

49 cm

4 cm

E4 Copy and complete this table to work out 7 × 28.

×	20	8
7		

E5 Copy and complete this table to work out 9 × 14.

×	10	...
9		

E6 Draw tables to work these out.

(a) 5 × 19   (b) 7 × 72   (c) 46 × 6   (d) 83 × 5

E7 Work out these multiplications without a calculator.

(a) 6 × 23   (b) 7 × 56   (c) 4 × 63   (d) 64 × 5

E8 A disco ticket costs £9 per person.
How much will 81 tickets cost?

E9 A woman spends £4 a week on the football pools.
How much is this over a 33 week football season?

E10 How many days are there in 48 weeks?

E11 Sam uses 42 litres of petrol a week.
How much is this over eight weeks?

E12 Copy and complete this table to work out 234 × 4.

×	200	30	4
4			

E13 Work these out.

(a) 124×2 (b) 103×3 (c) 205×2 (d) 150×3

E14 Work these out.

(a) 5×141 (b) 128×6 (c) 307×3 (d) 216×4

E15 You need to use the following facts.

Eiffel Tower
321 metres high

Saturn V Rocket
364 feet tall

Statue of Liberty
93 metres high

Empire State Building
381 metres high

Scuba diver
6 feet long

(a) A blue whale can be as long as 18 scuba divers.

How long can a blue whale be?

(b) Yosemite waterfall is nearly 8 times
as high as the Statue of Liberty.

Find the height of Yosemite waterfall.

(c) The Grand Canyon is nearly as deep as a
stack of 7 Empire State Buildings.

How deep is the Grand Canyon?

(d) The ice cap over the South Pole is nearly as deep as
a stack of 9 Eiffel Towers.

How deep is the ice cap?

(e) The Petronas Towers in Kuala Lumpur
are 4 times as tall as a Saturn V Rocket.

How tall are the Petronas Towers?

F Tables to multiply

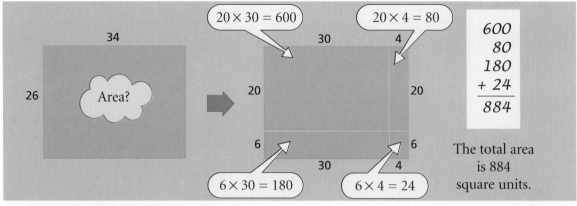

$20 \times 30 = 600$ $20 \times 4 = 80$

600
80
180
+ 24
884

$6 \times 30 = 180$ $6 \times 4 = 24$

The total area is 884 square units.

×	30	4
20	600	80
6	180	24

$26 \times 34 = ?$

600
80
180
+ 24
$26 \times 34 = 884$

F1 (a) Copy and complete this table.

(b) Use the table to work out 47×25.

(c) Make a table for 46×26 and work it out.

×	20	5
40		
7		

F2 Work out 37×24 by filling in a table like this.

×	20	4
30		
7		

F3 Make tables for these multiplications and use them to work out the answers.

(a) 19×16 (b) 13×27 (c) 21×34 (d) 45×25

(e) 15×15 (f) 23×91 (g) 96×41 (h) 62×87

F4 In a school hall the seats are laid out in 21 equal rows.
There are 16 seats in each row. How many seats are there altogether?

F5 Andrea took part in a sponsored swim. She was sponsored £23 for each length.
She completed 37 lengths. How much sponsor money should she collect?

F6 Find the area of a rectangle that measures 56 cm by 22 cm.

Three digits   an investigation

- You have three digits: 3, 4, 6.
  Make as many different multiplications
  as you can of the form ☐☐ × ☐.
  You must use all three digits.

  34×6 63×4

  Which one gives the largest result? Which gives the smallest?

- Investigate for different sets of digits.
  Can you say how to get the largest and smallest results for
  any set of three digits?

Four digits   an investigation

- You have four digits: 1, 2, 3, 4.

  How many different multiplications can you make
  of the form ☐☐ × ☐☐ ?

  14×32
  12×34 21×34

  Which gives the largest result? Which gives the smallest?

- Can you find the largest and smallest results for the digits 2, 3, 4, 5?

- Investigate for different sets of digits.
  Can you say how to get the largest and smallest results with any set of four digits?

What progress have you made?

Statement

Evidence

I can multiply and divide numbers
by 10, 100 and 1000.

1 Write down the results of these.
   (a) 405×100 (b) 340×10 (c) 10×600
   (d) $300 \div 100$ (e) $210 \div 10$ (f) $3500 \div 100$

I can do multiplications like
3×40 and 5×60.

2 Write down the results of these.
   (a) 3×40 (b) 5×60 (c) 6×30
   (d) 20×80 (e) 50×7 (f) 30×40

I can do multiplications like
47×6 without a calculator.

3 Work these out without a calculator.
   (a) 47×6 (b) 4×38 (c) 7×902
   (d) 3×84 (e) 55×6 (f) 318×4

I can do multiplications like
27×36 without a calculator.

4 Work these out without a calculator.
   (a) 27×36 (b) 16×32 (c) 21×43
   (d) 72×31 (e) 82×27 (f) 57×63

16 Balancing

This work will help you solve simple balance puzzles.

A Scales

1

2

B Balance pictures

The scales balance in these pictures.
Find the weight of each animal.

B1 (a)

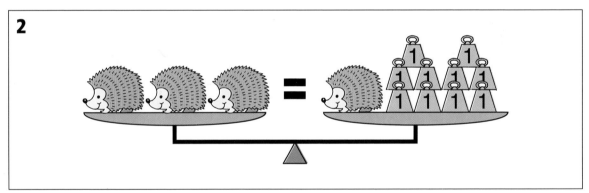

(b)

B2 These scales balance.
Find the weight of each animal.

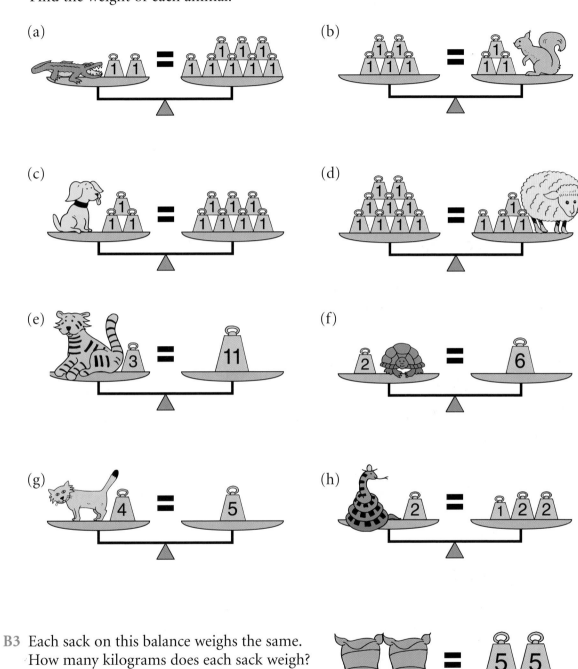

(a)

(b)

(c)

(d)

(e)

(f)

(g)

(h)

B3 Each sack on this balance weighs the same.
How many kilograms does each sack weigh?

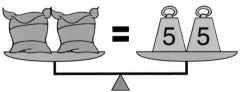

B4 Work out the weight of each of these objects.

(a)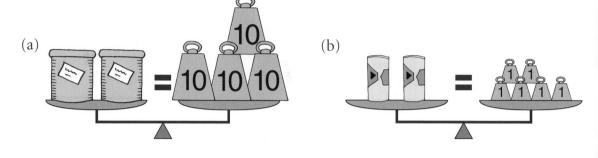

(b)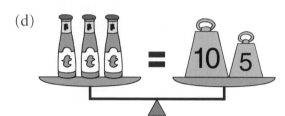

(c)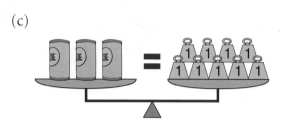

(d)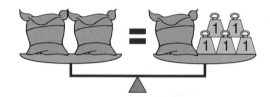

B5 Find the weight of one of these sacks.
(Hint: try taking a sack off each side.)

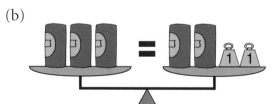

B6 Find the weight of a tin in each of these pictures.

(a)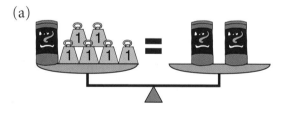

(b)

(c)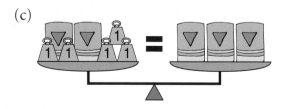

(d)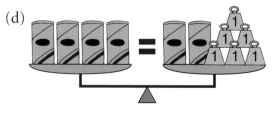

B7 Find the weight of one of these tins.
(Hint: first you need to take some
weights off each side.)

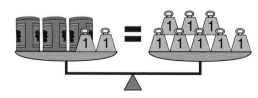

B8 Find the weight of a tin in each of these pictures.

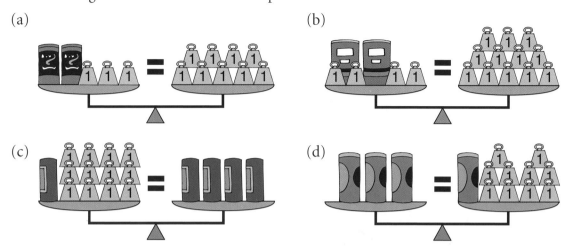

(a)

(b)

(c)

(d)

B9 Make up a balance puzzle picture and give it
to someone else to solve.

B10 Draw a balance puzzle picture, and write out an explanation
of how you solve it.

You may want to make a poster of your explanation.

What progress have you made?

Statement

I can solve a picture balance puzzle.

Evidence

1 Find the weight of a goose in this picture.

2 Draw a balance puzzle of your own and then
solve it.

⑰ Oral questions: money 1

T

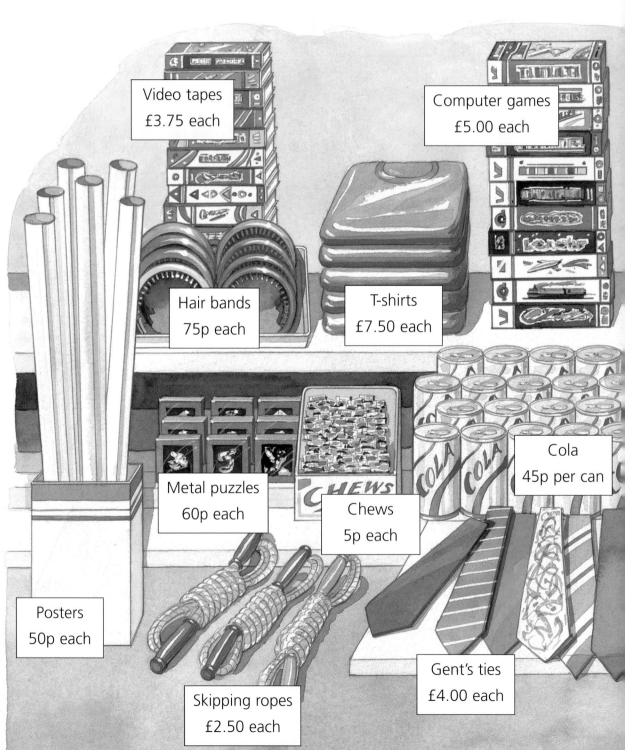

Video tapes
£3.75 each

Computer games
£5.00 each

Hair bands
75p each

T-shirts
£7.50 each

Cola
45p per can

Metal puzzles
60p each

Chews
5p each

Posters
50p each

Skipping ropes
£2.50 each

Gent's ties
£4.00 each

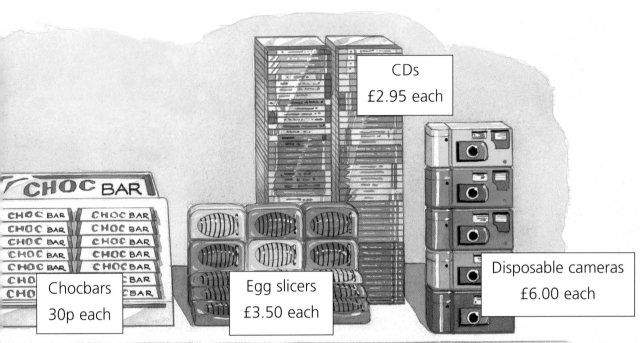

CDs
£2.95 each

Disposable cameras
£6.00 each

Chocbars
30p each

Egg slicers
£3.50 each

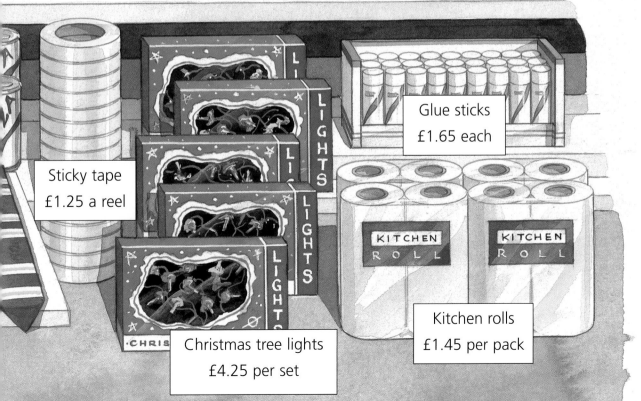

Glue sticks
£1.65 each

Sticky tape
£1.25 a reel

Kitchen rolls
£1.45 per pack

Christmas tree lights
£4.25 per set

105

⑱ Gravestones

This is about looking at data, displaying it and
drawing conclusions.
The work will help you

◆ find information from a table

◆ draw a grouped frequency chart

◆ decide which sort of chart is best for the data

◆ use data to test a hypothesis

A What gravestones tell us

Graveyards can be very interesting places.
Gravestones (if they can be read!) tell us

> the person's name
>
> the date when they died
>
> how old they were

Gravestones have even been used to study the growth of moss!
The data on a gravestone tells us when it was put up.

Amy and Holly live in Manchester.
They are working together on a
history project.

It is about an old family called the
Robinsons. Most of them are
buried in St Mary's Church in
Cheadle.

Amy and Holly went to the church
and made a list of all the Robinson
gravestones.

First names	Date when they died	Age
William	18 December 1832	54
John	24 January 1776	56
John Hanson	11 April 1798	4
Richard	29 July 1821	63
Jane	24 November 1827	68
Thomas	23 October 1790	69
Catherine	11 July 1793	71
Catherine	4 November 1757	2
Ann	26 August 1766	1
Frances	7 June 1772	6
Harriet	10 November 1813	1
Anne	16 March 1816	2
Hannah	5 March 1830	40
Martha	14 June 1846	57

A1 When was a Robinson first buried in St Mary's?

A2 For how many years were the Robinsons buried there?

A3 Amy says that most of the Robinsons seemed to die in winter. What do you think?

B Making a frequency table

Holly was interested in the ages at which the Robinsons died.
She decided to make a **frequency table**.

Here is how she started …

Why is this not a good way to show the data?

It is better to **group** the ages.

Age (in years)	Tally	Frequency
0–9		
10–19		
20–29		
30–39		
40–49		
50–59		
60–69		
70–79		

Age (in years)	Tally	Frequency
1	II	
2	II	
3		
4	I	
5		
6	I	
7		
8		
9		
10		
11		
12		
13		
14		

B1 Copy and complete the grouped frequency table.
Does it show anything interesting about the ages at which people died?
Jot down anything you notice.

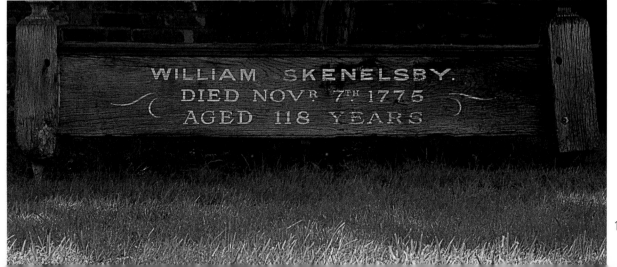

WILLIAM SKENELSBY.
DIED NOVR 7TH 1775
AGED 118 YEARS

C Comparing charts

For work in pairs

These graphs were drawn on a computer.
Each graph shows the data about the Robinson graves.

C1 This is a frequency bar chart.

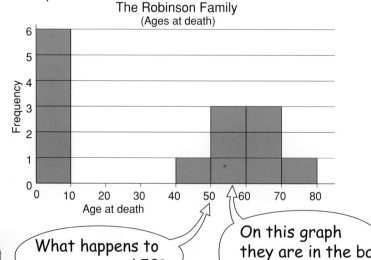

Are there some bars missing here?

C2 This is also a frequency bar chart, but the age groups are marked differently.

What happens to someone aged 50?

On this graph they are in the bar to the <u>right</u>.

Which group does someone aged 70 go in, 60–70 or 70–80?

C3 This is a pie chart.

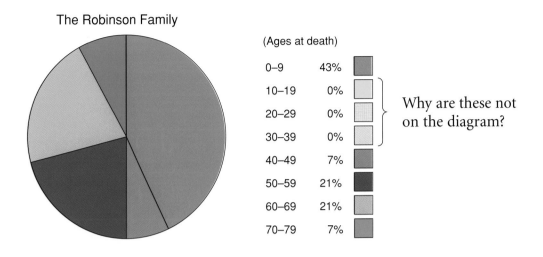

The Robinson Family

(Ages at death)

0–9	43%	
10–19	0%	
20–29	0%	
30–39	0%	
40–49	7%	
50–59	21%	
60–69	21%	
70–79	7%	

Why are these not on the diagram?

C4 Which chart best shows each of these?

(a) Almost half the Robinsons died before they reached ten years old.

(b) None of the Robinsons died between 10 and 39 years old.

(c) There are 14 Robinsons buried in St Mary's churchyard.

D Drawing a frequency chart

Frequency charts are useful for displaying a lot of data.
They can make it easier to see what is going on.

> **D1** This question is on sheet 94.

What progress have you made?

Statement

I can understand a frequency chart.

I can make a grouped frequency table.

Evidence

1

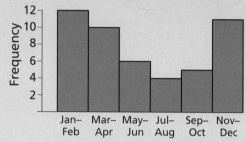

Bar chart showing when people died

(a) How many died in January and February?

(b) How many gravestones were recorded?

(c) In which months did fewest people die?

2 Here are some people's estimates of the length of a line, in cm.

6	11	10	19	12	10	14	30
12	14	21	12	17	6	24	16
19	15	12	21	7	11	13	14
13	15	22	14	14	13		

Copy and complete this grouped frequency table.

Estimate (cm)	Tally	Frequency
5–9		
10–14		
15–19		
20–24		
25–29		
30–34		

 **Brackets**

This is about using brackets in expressions.
The work will help you

◆ use brackets to show which part of a calculation is done first

◆ work out the value of expressions that use brackets

A Check it out

Mrs Turner's class were given some homework to do.
They had to make some **expressions** that gave 24.
Here are some of their homeworks.

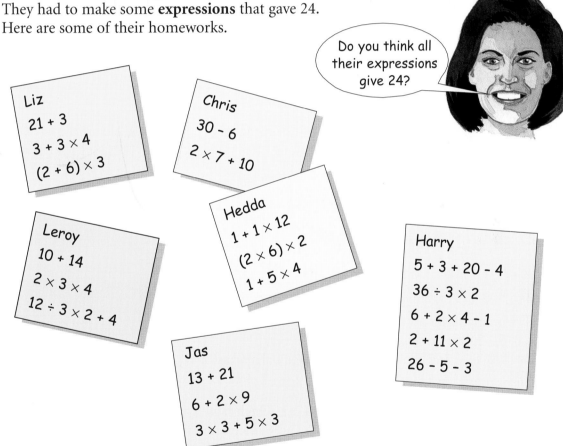

Do you think all their expressions give 24?

Liz
21 + 3
3 + 3 × 4
(2 + 6) × 3

Chris
30 – 6
2 × 7 + 10

Hedda
1 + 1 × 12
(2 × 6) × 2
1 + 5 × 4

Leroy
10 + 14
2 × 3 × 4
12 ÷ 3 × 2 + 4

Harry
5 + 3 + 20 – 4
36 ÷ 3 × 2
6 + 2 × 4 – 1
2 + 11 × 2
26 – 5 – 3

Jas
13 + 21
6 + 2 × 9
3 × 3 + 5 × 3

● You could make your own list of expressions that give 24.

Ask a friend to check them.

111

A1 Work these out without using a calculator.

(a) $(3 + 1) \times 2$ (b) $5 + (2 \times 4)$ (c) $(8 - 3) \times 2$

(d) $8 + (3 \times 5)$ (e) $16 + (8 \div 2)$ (f) $(20 - 10) \div 5$

(g) $15 + (15 \div 3)$ (h) $(2 \times 3) - 6$ (i) $(5 - 2) \times (3 + 1)$

(j) $(12 - 6) \div 2$ (k) $12 - (6 \div 2)$ (l) $18 - (5 \times 3)$

A2 Copy these calculations.
Use brackets to show which part of the calculation is done first.

(a) $6 - 1 \times 3 = 15$ (b) $4 \times 1 + 2 = 12$ (c) $2 + 1 \times 5 = 15$

(d) $6 \div 3 + 9 = 11$ (e) $2 + 3 \times 4 = 14$ (f) $5 \times 2 - 1 = 5$

(g) $5 - 1 \times 4 = 16$ (h) $2 + 2 \times 2 = 6$ (i) $3 \times 3 - 3 = 0$

(j) $4 + 4 \div 4 = 2$ (k) $12 \div 3 \times 2 = 2$ (l) $10 - 6 - 2 = 6$

A3 Sort these into three matching pairs.

A Add 2 and 3 then multiply the result by 7.   X $2 \times (3 + 7)$

B Multiply 7 by 2 then add 3 to the result.   Y $(2 + 3) \times 7$

C Add 3 and 7 then multiply the result by 2.   Z $(7 \times 2) + 3$

A4 Find the missing numbers to make these calculations correct.

(a) $(1 + \square) \times 2 = 10$ (b) $(\square - 2) \times 4 = 12$

(c) $(3 \times \square) - 5 = 4$ (d) $2 \times (10 - \square) = 4$

(e) $4 \times (\square - 3) = 40$ (f) $(6 + \square) \div 3 = 5$

(g) $9 \div (\square + 4) = 1$ (h) $10 \div (6 - \square) = 2$

(i) $20 \div (\square + 6) = 2$ (j) $(4 \times 3) - (5 - \square) = 9$

A5 How many different numbers can you find using
2, 3, 5, +, × and one set of brackets?
Use 2, 3, 5, + and × exactly once in each calculation.

For example $(5 + 2) \times 3 = 21$

A6 Make up as many expressions as you can which have a value of 4.
In each expression use the digits 2, 4 and 6 once only.
You can use any of +, −, ×, ÷ and brackets as often as you like.

Three in a row a game for two or more players

What you need

- You need three dice.
  You also need to make a copy of the game board shown below.

When it is your turn

- Roll the three dice.

- Use the numbers and brackets to make an expression that has a value on the board.

- Write down your calculation for the other players to check. They can challenge you and get a free go if your calculation is incorrect or hasn't got any brackets.

7	8	9	10
6	1	2	11
5	4	3	12
16	15	14	13

- If you are correct you cross out the value of the expression on the board (or cover it with a counter).

The winner

- The winner is the first player to cross out three numbers in a row (across, down or diagonally).

B Brackets galore!

B1 Expressions may have more than one set of brackets.
Without using a calculator, work out the value of these expressions.

$$(2 + 3) \times (10 - 3) \qquad ((4 \times 20) \div 2) \times 5$$

$$(10 - (2 + 5)) \times 3 \qquad 8 + (2 \times (4 + 6))$$

B2 You can use brackets to give different values
for the expression $5 + 3 \times 4 - 1$.

For example, $((5 + 3) \times 4) - 1 = 31$.

Find as many different values as you can for

(a) $5 + 3 \times 4 - 1$ (b) $12 \div 2 + 4 \times 2$

Pam's game for two or more players

- You need a dice.
  Each player copies the board below.

- Roll the dice six times.
- Everyone puts the numbers in their squares from left to right.
- Use brackets and +, −, × or ÷ between your squares to get as close to 100 as you can.
- Score 3 for a direct hit, 2 if you are between 95 and 105, 1 for 90 to 100.

Example

5, 3, 6, 3, 6, 6 are rolled.

⬚5⬚ ⬚3⬚ ⬚6⬚ ⬚3⬚ ⬚6⬚ ⬚6⬚ =

Jo writes

$((5 + 3) \times 6) + ((3 + 6) \times 6) = 102$

She scores 2.

Can you do better?

What progress have you made?

Statement	Evidence

I can work out expressions that use brackets.

1 Work these out.
  (a) $(7 \times 2) + 1$ (b) $(1 + 4) \times 2$
  (c) $(20 + 10) \div 3$ (d) $5 \times (7 - 3)$
  (e) $8 \div (1 + 3)$ (f) $(1 \times 2) + (3 \times 4)$

I can use brackets in expressions.

2 Copy these calculations and use brackets to show which part of the calculation is done first.
  (a) $6 + 1 \times 2 = 14$
  (b) $3 \times 10 - 8 = 6$
  (c) $10 - 6 \div 2 = 7$

I can use more than one set of brackets.

3 Work these out without a calculator.
  (a) $(3 + 5) \times (7 - 2)$
  (b) $(20 - (6 + 7)) \times 2$

Review 2

Do not use a calculator in this review.

1 Write down the coordinates of each corner of this shape.

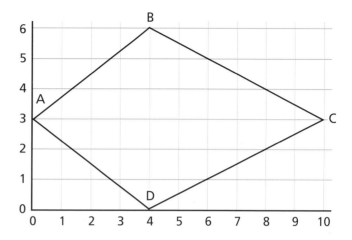

2 The points P, Q and R are three corners of a square.

(a) What are the coordinates of the fourth corner of the square?

(b) What are the coordinates of the point halfway between P and Q?

(c) What are the coordinates of the point halfway between Q and R?

(d) What are the coordinates of the point which is at the centre of the square?

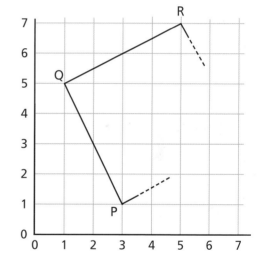

3 (a) What is the perimeter of this shape?

(b) What is the area of the shape?

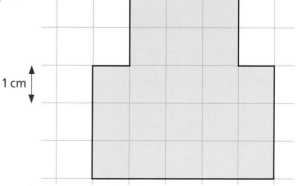

1 cm

4 (a) Draw a sketch of this L-shape.

   (b) Work out the two missing lengths
       and mark them on your sketch.

   (c) Split the L-shape into rectangles.
       Use this to work out the area of the whole shape.

   (d) Work out the perimeter of the L-shape.

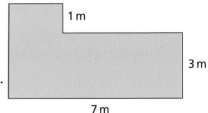

5 Use this number line to help you find the nearest ten to
   (a) 1788   (b) 1772   (c) 1803   (d) 1798   (e) 1809

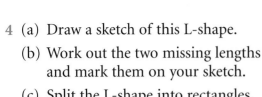

6 What is the nearest ten to each of these numbers?
   (a) 5132   (b) 4671   (c) 2598   (d) 3601
   (e) 1059   (f) 3749   (g) 6699   (h) 1008

7 Use this number line to help you find the nearest hundred to
   (a) 24 860   (b) 24 820   (c) 25 080   (d) 24 990   (e) 25 150

8 Round each of these numbers to the nearest hundred.
   (a) 3452   (b) 7633   (c) 8558   (d) 2996   (e) 1950

9 Round each of these numbers to the nearest thousand.
   (a) 17 546   (b) 18 934   (c) 16 511   (d) 18 500   (e) 19 500

10 Round 18 752 to
   (a) the nearest 10   (b) the nearest hundred   (c) the nearest thousand

11 Write down the results of these multiplications.
   (a) 34 × 10   (b) 34 × 100   (c) 234 × 100   (d) 405 × 10   (e) 100 × 54

12 Copy and complete these multiplications.
   (a) ? × 100 = 31 000   (b) 120 × ? = 1200   (c) ? × 1000 = 50 000

13 Change these to centimetres.

    (a) 6 metres   (b) 38 metres   (c) 150 metres (d) 900 metres

14 Change these to metres.

    (a) 800 cm   (b) 1200 cm   (c) 2000 cm   (d) 35 000 cm

15 Work these out.

    (a) 20×40 (b) 30×60 (c) 20×300 (d) 500×30 (e) 60×60

16 Work these out.

    (a) 4×26 (b) 213×4 (c) 23×34 (d) 62×43 (e) 18×67

17 (a) Find the area of a rectangle that measures 23 cm by 45 cm.

    (b) Chairs cost £36 each. How much do 14 cost?

    (c) A box is 65 cm tall. How tall are 18 boxes on top of one another?

18 Each of these scales balances. The weights are in kilograms.
Find the weight of a tin in each picture.

    (a)   (b)

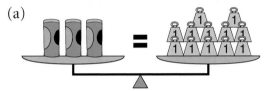 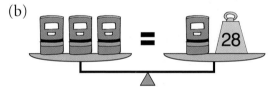

19 (a) Work out the weight of a brick.   (b) Work out the weight of a bottle.

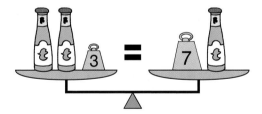

20 Work these out.

    (a) $5 + (3 \times 4)$ (b) $13 - (4 - 1)$ (c) $(3 + 4) \times 2$ (d) $24 - (8 \div 2)$

21 Copy these calculations and use brackets to show
which part is done first.

    (a) $2 \times 5 + 3 = 16$ (b) $20 - 10 \div 2 = 5$ (c) $20 - 10 \div 2 = 15$

22 Work out the missing numbers.

    (a) $(5 + \square) \div 2 = 4$ (b) $12 - (\square + 1) = 3$ (c) $6 \times (\square - 1) = 30$

20 Lines at right angles

This work will help you find right angles and draw them.

A Thinking about right angles

A1 The 8 and 5 on this clock face are joined to the centre.

The angle at the centre is a right angle.

What other pairs of numbers make a right angle?

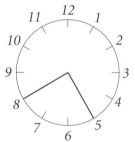

A2 Make a sketch of the eight points of the compass (north, north-east, ...).

(a) Jenny is facing west.
She turns through a right angle clockwise.
What direction is she facing now?

(b) Peter is facing south-east.
He turns through a right angle anticlockwise.
What direction is he facing now?

(c) Amal is facing north-west.
She turns through a right angle clockwise.
What direction is she facing now?

118

B Drawing and checking right angles

A **set square** helps you draw accurate right angles.

Practise drawing some right angles with a set square.

B1 A rectangle has a right angle at each of its four corners.
Follow these instructions to draw a rectangle 9 cm wide by 6 cm high.

1 Draw a line 9 cm long.

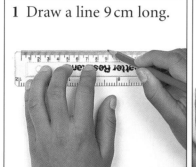

2 At one end, draw a line at right angles.

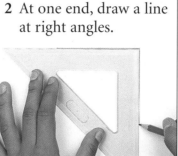

3 Do the same at the other end.

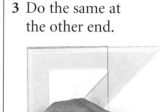

4 Put a mark 6 cm down each of these two lines.

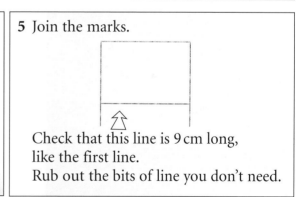

5 Join the marks.

Check that this line is 9 cm long, like the first line.
Rub out the bits of line you don't need.

B2 This is a sketch of a rectangle.
Draw the rectangle accurately.

This means a right angle.

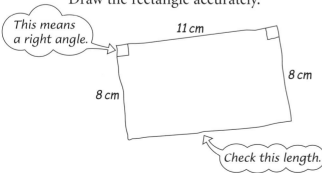

11 cm

8 cm

8 cm

Check this length.

B3 Draw this shape accurately.

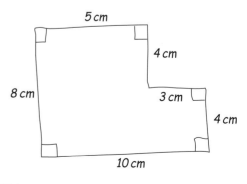

5 cm

4 cm

8 cm

3 cm

4 cm

10 cm

B4 Draw a shape of your own with right angles at all its corners.

B5 Line *a* is at right angles to line *b*.
We say that line *a* is **perpendicular** to line *b*.
Check this with a set square.

Some other pairs of lines are perpendicular.
Find the pairs.
Try to decide without a set square.
Then check with a set square.
If the lines are far apart, use the corner
of a piece of paper to check.

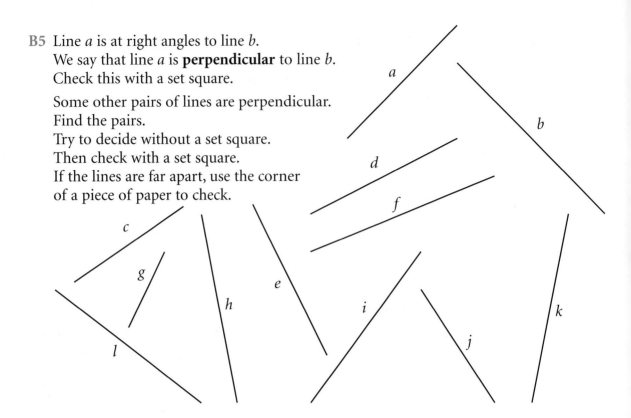

B6 Just by looking, decide which of the corners are right angles.

Now check with a set square.

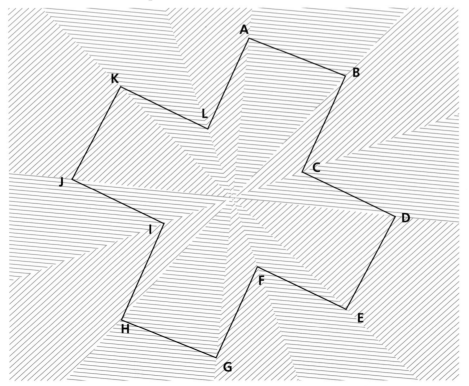

What progress have you made?

Statement

I can find right angles.

Evidence

1 Which lines are at right angles to one another here?

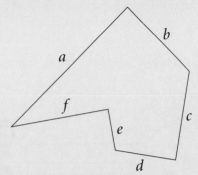

2 Use the corner of a piece of paper to decide which pairs of lines are perpendicular.

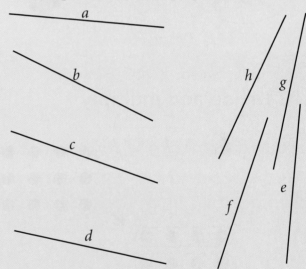

I can draw a shape with right angles accurately.

3 Draw this shape accurately.

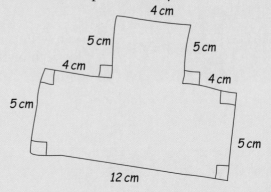

 **Division**

This work will help you

◆ understand how division is related to multiplication

◆ improve your skills in dividing

A Sharing

15 sweets are shared equally between 3 people.　　Each person gets 5 sweets.

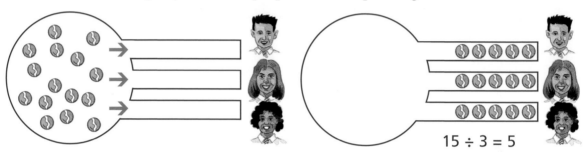

$15 \div 3 = 5$

B Divide and multiply

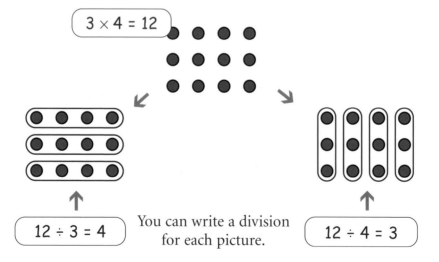

$3 \times 4 = 12$

$12 \div 3 = 4$

You can write a division for each picture.

$12 \div 4 = 3$

B1 This diagram starts with $2 \times 4 = 8$.

Copy and complete the two divisions.

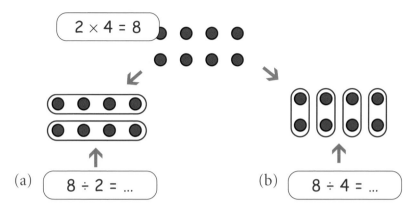

(a) $8 \div 2 = \ldots$

(b) $8 \div 4 = \ldots$

B2 For each diagram, copy and complete the calculations.

(a)
$3 \times 2 = 6$
$6 \div 3 = \ldots$
$6 \div 2 = \ldots$

(b)
$3 \times 5 = 15$
$15 \div 3 = \ldots$
$15 \div 5 = \ldots$

(c)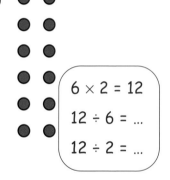
$6 \times 2 = 12$
$12 \div 6 = \ldots$
$12 \div 2 = \ldots$

B3 Copy and complete each set of calculations.

(a)
$3 \times 8 = 24$
$24 \div 3 = \ldots$

(b)
$5 \times 5 = 25$
$25 \div 5 = \ldots$

(c)
$4 \times \ldots = 24$
$24 \div 4 = \ldots$

B4 Work these out.

(a) $16 \div 4$　　(b) $16 \div 2$　　(c) $9 \div 3$　　(d) $35 \div 5$

(e) $18 \div 9$　　(f) $33 \div 3$　　(g) $18 \div 2$　　(h) $28 \div 7$

B5 Find the missing numbers.

(a) $28 \div \blacksquare = 7$　　(b) $30 \div \blacksquare = 6$　　(c) $8 \div \blacksquare = 2$　　(d) $\blacksquare \div 4 = 8$

C Grouping

Sarah packs 15 buns in boxes of 3.
How many boxes will she fill?

 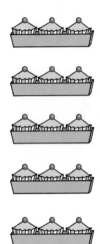

She fills 5 boxes.

C1 Joe has 12 cakes.
He puts them in bags, 2 in each bag.
How many bags does he use?

C2 Kiri has 15 apples.
She puts them in bags, 5 in each bag.
How many bags does she use?

C3 Pat has 30 eggs.
She puts them in boxes of 6.
How many boxes does she fill?

C4 Some oranges are sold in packs of 4.
How many packs can be made from
16 oranges?

C5 Jane has 12 cans of cola.
She puts them in boxes of 6.
How many boxes does she fill?

C6 Bags of grapefruit hold 3 each.
How many bags are needed to pack
21 grapefruit?

C7 Sam pays for his bus fare with 5p
coins. The fare is 35p.
How many coins does he use?

C8 Sarah's panther eats 8 tins of cat food
every day.
How long will 80 tins last?

C9 Dee packs biscuits in packs of 7.
How many packs will she make with
35 biscuits?

C10 Ken's fish eats 2 boxes of fish food
every day.
How long will 50 boxes last?

C11 Doughnuts are packed in boxes of 4.
How many boxes will be filled from 32
doughnuts?

C12 Gerry eats 3 chocolate bars each week.
How long will 36 bars last?

D Sharing and grouping

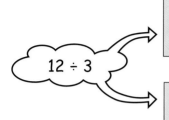

Share 12 cakes equally between 3 people.
How many cakes for each person?

Pack 12 cakes in boxes of 3.
How many boxes do you need?

D1 20 cakes are shared equally between 5 people.
How many cakes does each person get?

D2 Chocolate bars are sold in packs of 2.
How many packs are made from 20 chocolate bars?

D3 4 people have a meal.
They share the cost equally.
The meal costs £40.
How much does each person pay?

D4 Calculate these.

(a) $21 \div 3$ (b) $16 \div 8$ (c) $24 \div 2$

(d) $36 \div 6$ (e) $32 \div 4$ (f) $30 \div 5$

(g) $45 \div 9$ (h) $64 \div 8$ (i) $72 \div 9$

D5 In these questions you decide whether
to add, subtract, multiply or divide.

(a) Joy sells 25 raffle tickets, her brother sells 17.
How many have they sold altogether?

(b) A taxi will carry 4 passengers.
How many taxis are needed to carry 24 people?

(c) A train at a fair has 4 coaches.
There are 8 seats in each coach.
How many people can the train carry?

(d) 30 chairs are put in rows, with 6 chairs in each row.
How many rows are there?

(e) In a car park, the spaces are in rows.
There are 5 rows with 10 spaces in each row.
How many spaces are there altogether?

E Remainders

Chocolate drops

Practical work is described in the teacher's guide.

Share 13 sweets equally between 3 people.

Each person gets 4 sweets.

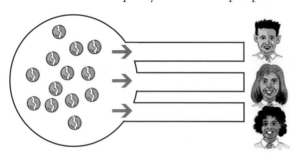

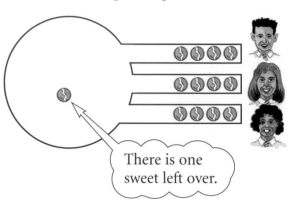

There is one sweet left over.

Pack 13 buns in packs of 3.

We can make 4 packs.

There is one bun left over.

We write **13 ÷ 3 = 4 remainder 1**.

E1 Work these out.

    (a) 9 ÷ 2   (b) 17 ÷ 3   (c) 22 ÷ 4   (d) 17 ÷ 5   (e) 33 ÷ 3

    (f) 11 ÷ 3   (g) 58 ÷ 10   (h) 18 ÷ 5   (i) 23 ÷ 4   (j) 16 ÷ 5

    (k) 20 ÷ 3   (l) 36 ÷ 4   (m) 35 ÷ 5   (n) 29 ÷ 3   (o) 22 ÷ 3

E2 Work these out.

    (a) 17 ÷ 6   (b) 47 ÷ 10   (c) 28 ÷ 6   (d) 23 ÷ 7   (e) 16 ÷ 8

    (f) 20 ÷ 9   (g) 30 ÷ 4   (h) 35 ÷ 7   (i) 29 ÷ 8   (j) 44 ÷ 6

E3 Share 14 oranges equally between 3 people.

    (a) How many oranges does each person get?

    (b) How many oranges are left over?

E4 Fiona puts 17 biscuits into bags of 4.

  (a) How many bags does she fill?

  (b) How many biscuits are left over?

E5 Kirsty has 27 eggs.
   She packs them in boxes, with 6 in each box.

  (a) How many boxes can she fill?

  (b) How many eggs are left over?

E6 29 apples are to be shared equally
   between 4 children.

  (a) How many apples does each child get?

  (b) How many are left over?

E7 Jamal puts 14 oranges into packs of 3.

  (a) How many packs can he fill?

  (b) How many oranges are left over?

E8 7 people want to share 24 coconuts equally.
   How many will each person get, and
   how many will be left over?

E9 3 children share a tube of fruit gums.
   There are 17 gums in the tube.
   How many gums does each child get,
   and how many are left over?

E10 On Carla's birthday, Gran gave her £15,
   Mum gave her £8 and Dad £5.
   She wants to buy some sketchpads.
   They cost £3 each.

  (a) How many can she buy?

  (b) How much money does she have left over?

E11 Some sweets are shared between 5 children.
   Each child gets 3 sweets and
   there are 2 sweets left over.
   How many sweets were there to start with?

Sharing puzzles

1 Can you share these six jewels
  between three people so each
  gets the same weight?
  No cutting!

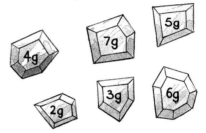

2 Can you share these nine
  jewels between two people
  so that each gets the same
  weight?

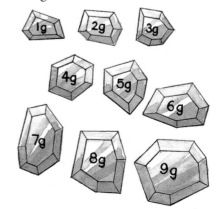

How about between three
people? Four? Five? …

F Division by a single-digit number: chunking

You can work out 215 ÷ 6 by finding how many 6s are in 215.

Start with 215.

Take off as many 'chunks' of 6s as you can.

We can take off
10 + 10 + 10 + 5 = 35
chunks of 6.

		215
10 × 6	–	60
		155
10 × 6	–	60
		95
10 × 6	–	60
		35
5 × 6	–	30
		5

So 215 ÷ 6 = 35 rem 5.

- Are there any other ways of working out 215 ÷ 6?

F1 Grapefruit are packed in bags of 3.
How many bags can be filled from 84 grapefruit?

F2 Chocolate biscuits are sold in packs of 5.
How many packs can be filled from 65 biscuits?

F3 Apples are packed in fours.
How many packs can be filled from 125 apples?
How many apples are left over?

F4 29 apples are to be shared equally between 6 children.
How many apples does each child get?
How many are left over?

F5 Cakes are packed in boxes of 8.
How many boxes can be filled from 204 cakes?
How many cakes are left over?

F6 3 children share 72 conkers equally.
How many conkers does each child get?

F7 5 teachers share 127 rulers.

(a) How many rulers does each teacher get?

(b) How many rulers are left over?

F8 Granny has 94 antique thimbles.
She shares them equally between her 6 grandchildren.
If there are any left over, they are given to the oldest grandchild, Pat.
How many thimbles does Pat get altogether?

F9 A toymaker needs 4 wheels for each toy truck she makes.
She has 54 wheels.
How many trucks is this enough for?

F10 Helga is decorating cakes for a party.
Each cake needs 5 cherries.
How many cakes can she decorate if she has 133 cherries?

F11 A teacher has 101 chocolates.
She shares them equally between 12 children and
eats the remaining ones herself.

How many chocolates does each child get?
How many chocolates are left over for the teacher?

F12 Make up a question similar to those above.
Give your question to someone else to do.
Check that their answer is right.

F13 In these questions, decide whether to add, subtract, multiply or divide.

(a) Joy sells 54 raffle tickets.
Her brother sells 27.
How many have they sold altogether?

(b) A train has 4 coaches with 32 seats in each coach.
How many people can the train carry?

(c) 156 chairs are put in rows, with 6 chairs in each row.
How many rows are there?

(d) On Carla's birthday, Gran gave her £25, Mum £17 and Dad £15.
She wants to buy some books.
They cost £4 each.
How many can she buy?

F14 Make up a problem in words to go with each of these calculations.

(a) $69 \div 8$ (b) $104 \div 9$ (c) $157 \div 6$

(d) $232 \div 5$ (e) $178 \div 3$ (f) $274 \div 9$

Work out the answer to each of your problems.

G What should we do about remainders?

For class or group discussion

> **1** Cakes are sold in boxes of 8.
> Wanda needs 74 cakes for a party.
> How many boxes does she need to buy?

> **2** Steve is making toy cars. Each car has 4 wheels.
> He has 83 wheels.
> How many cars does he have enough for?

> **3** 67 children are going to the seaside by taxi.
> Each taxi carries 5 children.
> How many taxis will be needed?

G1 Saul is packing oranges in bags.
5 oranges go in each bag. He has 127 oranges.
How many bags can he fill?

G2 A lorry carries 9 tons of sand. There are 156 tons to be carried.
How many journeys will the lorry have to make?

G3 In a school dining hall, 10 children sit round each table.
At the Christmas party, there will be 282 children.
How many tables will be needed?

G4 Egg boxes hold 6 eggs.
How many boxes can be filled from 103 eggs?

G5 A baker can get 8 loaves into his oven at a time.
How many times will he need to use the oven to bake 150 loaves?

G6 Make up a division problem, using the numbers 73 and 5.
Give it to someone to solve.
See what they do about the remainder.

G7 Brian is making toy boxes.
Each box needs 8 screws, 2 hinges and 4 wheels.
Brian has 124 screws, 41 hinges and 103 wheels.
How many toy boxes will he be able to finish?

What progress have you made?

Statement	Evidence

I can use tables facts to divide when there is no remainder.

1 Write down the results of these.

   (a) $28 \div 4$ (b) $30 \div 5$ (c) $15 \div 3$

2 Work these out.

   (a) $42 \div 6$ (b) $36 \div 9$ (c) $64 \div 8$

I can use table facts to divide when there is a remainder.

3 Write down the results of these.

   (a) $26 \div 3$ (b) $33 \div 5$ (c) $29 \div 4$

4 Work these out.

   (a) $26 \div 6$ (b) $30 \div 7$ (c) $18 \div 8$

I can solve problems using division.

5 Solve these problems.

   (a) Share 13 buns equally between 3 boys.
      How many buns does each boy get?
      How many are left over?

   (b) Pens are packed in boxes of 6.
      How many boxes can be
      filled from 34 pens?
      How many pens are left over?

I can divide by a single-digit number without a calculator.

6 Work these out.

   (a) $147 \div 2$ (b) $238 \div 4$ (c) $303 \div 5$

7 Work these out.

   (a) $311 \div 6$ (b) $208 \div 7$ (c) $129 \div 9$

I know what to do about remainders when I solve a problem.

8 Solve these problems.

   (a) 178 people are queuing for taxis.
      Each taxi holds 4 passengers.
      How many taxis will be needed?

   (b) Tennis balls are packed in boxes of 6.
      How many boxes can be filled from 107
      balls?

22 Parallel lines

This work will help you draw and find parallel lines.

A Looking for parallel lines

T

A1 Look at line *a*.

   (a) One of the other lines is parallel to it.
       Which one is it?

   (b) One of the lines is perpendicular to *a*.
       Which one is it?

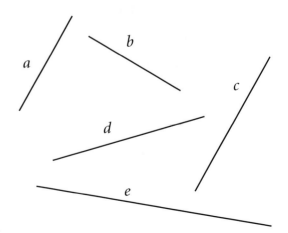

A2 (a) Which of the lines *v*, *w*, *x* or *y* is parallel to line *u*?

(b) There is another pair of parallel lines in the diagram. Which lines are they?

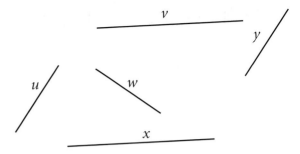

A3 True or false?

(a) A square has two pairs of parallel sides.

(b) A triangle can have one pair of parallel sides.

(c) A hexagon can have three pairs of parallel sides.

A4 There are three pairs of parallel lines in this shape. Which are they?

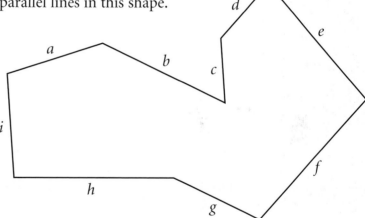

A5 Which of the lines *b*, *c* or *d* is parallel to line *a*? How can you be sure?

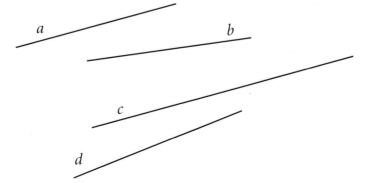

133

B Drawing parallel lines

1 Put a mark on the edge of a piece of paper near its corner.

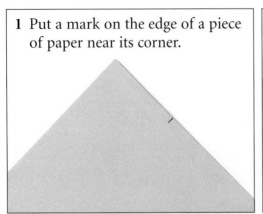

2 Draw a straight line and put the piece of paper along it. Draw against the first mark.

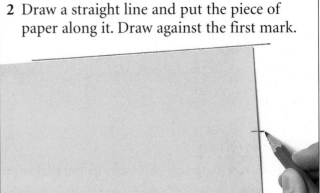

3 Slide the piece of paper along the line. Draw against the mark again.

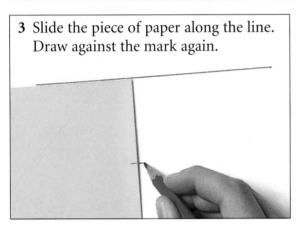

4 Join the two marks with a straight line.

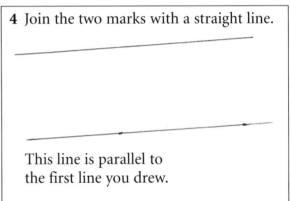

This line is parallel to the first line you drew.

You can make your lines 5 cm apart, for example, by using a ruler.

Measure 5 cm from the edge of the paper.

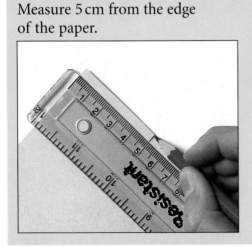

Then do the same as you did above.

B1 Answer the questions on sheet 152.

You can get a set of parallel lines by making several marks on your piece of paper.

This method is good for making designs like the ones below.

You can draw some like them or make parallel line designs of your own.

Work on plain paper.

Use a pencil so you can rub out some lines if you need to.

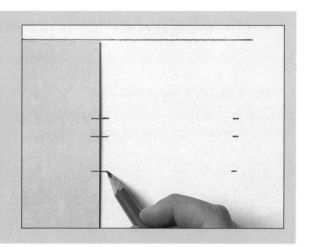

Start by drawing the outside four-sided shape.

C Checking whether lines are parallel

You can use the corner of a piece of paper to check that two lines are parallel.

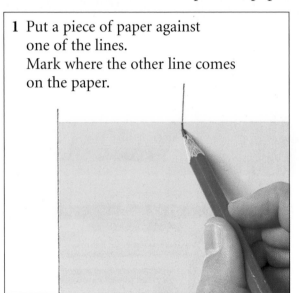

1 Put a piece of paper against one of the lines.
Mark where the other line comes on the paper.

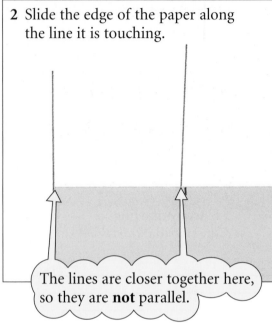

2 Slide the edge of the paper along the line it is touching.

The lines are closer together here, so they are **not** parallel.

C1 Do the questions on sheet 153.

C2 Are the two black lines parallel?

What progress have you made?

Statement

I can draw parallel lines.

I can check whether lines are parallel.

Evidence

1 Draw two parallel lines 6 cm apart.

2 Check whether these two lines are parallel.

This work will help you
◆ calculate with time
◆ use the 24-hour clock

A Happiness graphs

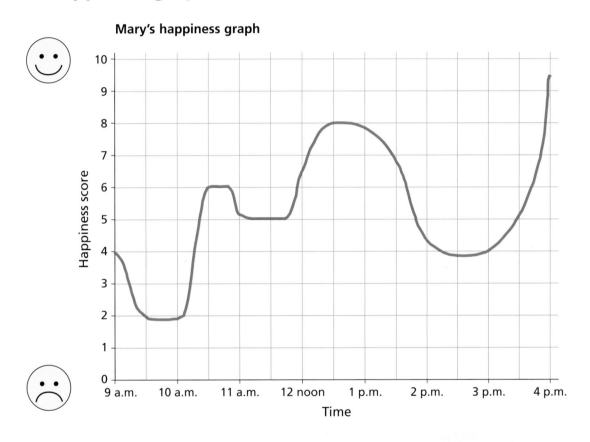

Mary's happiness graph

B Time planner

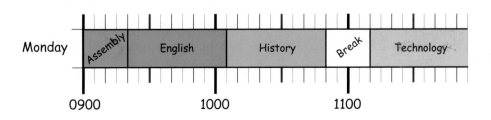

C At the same time

D Time lines

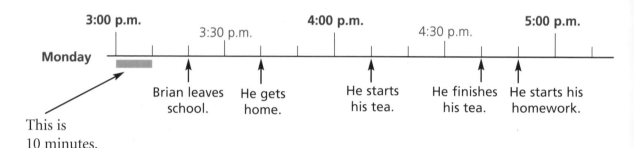

This is
10 minutes.

D1 What time does Brian leave school?

D2 What time does he get home?

D3 How long does it take him to get home?

D4 What time does he start his tea?

D5 How long does he take to eat his tea?

D6 What time does he start his homework?

D7 Brian spends 40 minutes on his homework.
What time does he finish it?

D8 How long is it between
   (a) getting home and starting his tea
   (b) getting home and starting his homework

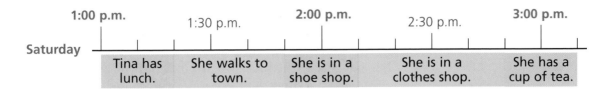

D9 Tina starts lunch at 1 o'clock. What time does she finish lunch?

D10 How long does it take Tina to walk to town?

D11 How long does she spend altogether in the shoe shop and the clothes shop?

D12 How long is it between finishing her lunch and having a cup of tea?

D13 After her cup of tea, Tina walks home. She takes 35 minutes to get home. What time does she get home?

E How long?

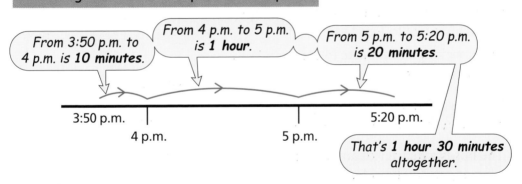

E1 How long is it
    (a) from 4:30 p.m. to 6:10 p.m.   (b) from 2:40 p.m. to 5:10 p.m.
    (c) from 8:20 a.m. to 11:10 a.m.   (d) from 11:30 a.m. to 1:20 p.m.

E2 How long is it
    (a) from a quarter to 7 to half past 8   (b) from half past 2 to 10 past 4
    (c) from 25 past 9 to 10 past 11   (d) from 10 past 8 to 20 to 10

E3 A film starts at 9:30 p.m. and finishes at 11:10 p.m. How long does it last?

E4 Sasha wants to go to a film. It starts at 8:20 p.m.
She leaves home at a quarter to 8.
How long has she got before the film starts?

Buses leave here at
8:15 a.m.
9:45 a.m.
11:10 a.m.
1:15 p.m.
4:05 p.m.

E5 Gary gets to the bus stop at 10:55 a.m.
How long does he have to wait for a bus?

E6 Sue gets to the bus stop at 12:40 p.m.
How long does she have to wait for a bus?

E7 Misha gets to the bus stop at a quarter to 4.
How long does he have to wait for a bus?

E8 Paul wants to see *Home Alone* at 2:15 p.m.
It takes him 30 minutes from home to the cinema.

What is the latest time he can leave home?

E9 Lana wants to see *Home Alone* at 4:10 p.m.
It will take her 45 minutes to get there.

What is the latest time she can leave?

MASCOT
Cinema

Home Alone

2:15 p.m.	4:10 p.m.
6:20 p.m.	8:45 p.m.

E10 Colin leaves home at 7:45 p.m.
It takes him 25 minutes to get to the cinema.

When he gets there, how long will he have to wait for the film to start?

E11 (a) How long does the bus take to get from
Market Hill to Red Lion?

(b) How long does it take to get from West Gate
to Flybridge?

E12 Roddy is at West Gate at half past 8.
How long does he have to wait for a bus?

E13 The bus is a quarter of an hour late
when it gets to Flybridge.

What time does it arrive at Flybridge?

TURBO BUS
timetable

Market Hill	8:10
Castle St	8:25
West Gate	8:40
York Road	9:00
Red Lion	9:25
Tay Cross	9:45
Oak Hill	10:05
Flybridge	10:20

F The 24-hour clock

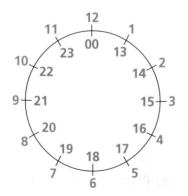

Flight	Destination	Time
FY36	Amsterdam	08:40
ZK23	Tashkent	10:55
MH65	Las Palmas	13:20
FY28	Paris CDG	15:50
AR15	Dubai	19:30
BR37	Aberdeen	23:00
DR98	Moscow	00:10

F1 Write these as 12-hour clock times using a.m. or p.m.

(a) 08:00   (b) 14:30   (c) 10:45   (d) 18:25   (e) 22:50

F2 Write these as 24-hour clock times.

(a) 8:30 a.m.   (b) 7:00 p.m.   (c) 11:30 a.m.   (d) 9:15 p.m.

(e) a quarter past midday   (f) half past midnight

F3 Copy and complete this table.

12-hour clock	24-hour clock
5 p.m.	
	16:30
11:30 a.m.	
	07:45
3:25 p.m.	
	21:20
10:35 p.m.	
	00:20

F4 The ferry from Castlebay to Oban in Scotland leaves at different times each day.

(a) At what time does the ferry leave Castlebay on a Tuesday?
Write your answer using a.m. or p.m.

(b) How long does the journey take on a Monday?

(c) Maddy is travelling on the ferry from Castlebay on Friday.
Her Dad says he will meet her in Oban at 11.30 p.m.
How long will Maddy have to wait for her Dad?

	Castlebay	Oban
	Depart	Arrive
Mon	0920	1435
Tues	1420	1930
Weds	0920	1435
Thurs	No service	
Fri	1650	2200

What progress have you made?

Statement	Evidence

I can work out how long it is between two times.

1 How long is it
(a) from half past 6 to a quarter past 7
(b) from 2:15 p.m. to 3:35 p.m.
(c) from 8:50 a.m. to 10:10 a.m.
(d) from 25 past 2 to 10 past 4

I can use the 24-hour clock.

2 Write these times using a.m. or p.m.
(a) 16:20   (b) 09:15   (c) 23:10

24 Work to rule

This is about finding rules for tile designs.
The work will help you find and use rules.

A Mobiles

Tom designs mobiles.
He makes the pieces with square glass tiles.

Tom uses a different design for the pieces in this mobile.

Questions A1 to A9 are all about this mobile design.

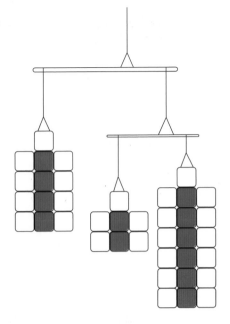

A1 Look at the piece that has 2 red tiles.
How many white tiles does it have?

A2 (a) Draw a piece that uses 3 red tiles.
(b) How many white tiles does it have?

A3 (a) Draw a piece that uses 5 red tiles.
(b) How many white tiles does it have?

A4 Copy and complete this table.

Number of red tiles	1	2	3	4	5	6
Number of white tiles				9		

A5 (a) Describe how the number of white tiles goes up
as the number of red tiles goes up.
(b) Explain why the number of white tiles goes up in this way.

A6 How many white tiles would you need for a piece with
(a) 8 red tiles   (b) 10 red tiles

A7 How many white tiles would you need for a piece
that has 100 red tiles?

A8 Explain how you can find the number of white tiles if you know
the number of red tiles.

A9 Work out how many white tiles you would need for a piece with
150 red tiles.

143

B Towers and L-shapes

Tom designs pieces for a different mobile.
He calls them 'towers'.

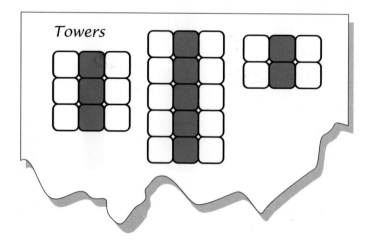

Towers

B1 How many white tiles are used for the piece with 5 red tiles?

B2 (a) Draw a tower that uses 6 red tiles.

(b) How many white tiles does it have?

B3 Copy and complete this table.

Towers						
Number of red tiles	1	2	3	4	5	6
Number of white tiles		4				

B4 (a) Without drawing, how many white tiles would you need for a tower that uses 8 red tiles?

(b) Check your result by drawing a tower that uses 8 red tiles.

B5 How many white tiles would you need for a tower with 15 red tiles?

B6 How many white tiles would you need for a tower with 40 red tiles?

B7 Explain how can you find the number of white tiles in a tower if you know the number of red tiles.

B8 Work out how many white tiles you would need for a tower with

(a) 100 red tiles   (b) 58 red tiles

Tom calls these designs 'L-shapes'.

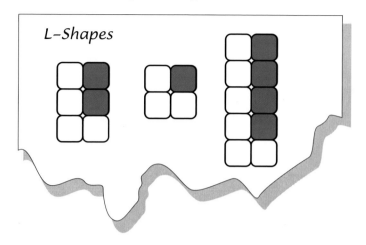

L–Shapes

B9 (a) Draw an L-shape that uses 5 red tiles.

(b) How many white tiles does it have?

B10 Copy and complete this table.

L-shapes						
Number of red tiles	1	2	3	4	5	6
Number of white tiles		4				

B11 (a) Without drawing, how many white tiles would you need for an L-shape that uses 9 red tiles?

(b) Check your result by drawing an L-shape that uses 9 red tiles.

B12 How many white tiles would you need for an L-shape with 26 red tiles?

B13 How many white tiles would you need for an L-shape with 100 red tiles?

B14 Explain how you can find the number of white tiles for an L-shape if you know the number of red tiles.

C Bridges

Tom designs pieces for another mobile.
He calls them 'bridges'.

Bridges

C1 How many white tiles are used for
the piece with 6 red tiles?

C2 (a) Draw a bridge that uses 2 red tiles.

(b) How many white tiles does it have?

C3 (a) Draw a bridge with 4 red tiles.

(b) How many white tiles does it have?

C4 How many **red** tiles are used for a piece with 7 **white** tiles?

C5 Copy and complete this table.

Bridges						
Number of red tiles	1	2	3	4	5	6
Number of white tiles	5					

C6 (a) Without drawing, how many white tiles would you need
for a bridge with 10 red tiles?

(b) Check your result by drawing a bridge with 10 red tiles.

C7 How many white tiles would you need for a bridge
with 20 red tiles?

C8 How many white tiles would you need for a bridge
with 50 red tiles?

C9

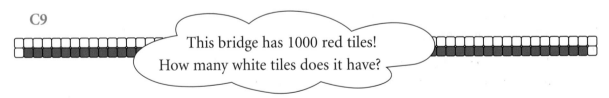

This bridge has 1000 red tiles!
How many white tiles does it have?

C10 Explain how you can find the number of white tiles for
a bridge if you know the number of red tiles.

C11 Work out how many white tiles you would need for a bridge with

(a) 25 red tiles (b) 36 red tiles

D Surrounds

Tom calls these designs 'surrounds'.

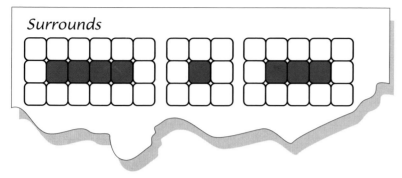

Surrounds

D1 (a) Draw a surround that uses 6 red tiles.

(b) How many white tiles does it have?

D2 Copy and complete this table.

Surrounds						
Number of red tiles	1	2	3	4	5	6
Number of white tiles			12			

D3 (a) Without drawing, how many white tiles would you need for a surround that uses 10 red tiles?

(b) Check your result by drawing a surround that uses 10 red tiles.

D4 How many white tiles would you need for a surround with 26 red tiles?

D5 How many white tiles would you need for a surround with 100 red tiles?

D6 Explain how you can find the number of white tiles for a surround if you know the number of red tiles.

E More designs

E1 There are four sets of designs below.
For each set of designs,

(a) find out how many white tiles you need for a piece
with 100 red tiles

(b) explain how you can find the number of white tiles
if you know the number of red tiles

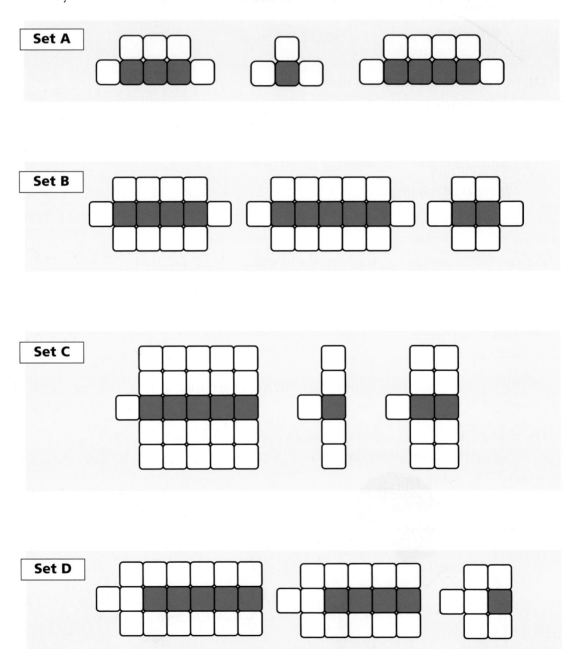

What progress have you made?

Statement

I can find and use rules, describing them in words.

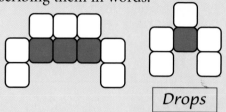

Drops

Evidence

These pieces are called 'drops'.

1 Look at the piece that has 4 red tiles. How many white tiles does it have?

2 (a) Draw the piece that uses 5 red tiles.

   (b) How many white tiles does it use?

3 Copy and complete this table for the drops.

Number of red tiles	1	2	3	4	5
Number of white tiles			7		

4 How many white tiles would you need for a piece with

   (a) 7 red tiles   (b) 10 red tiles

5 How many white tiles would you need for a piece with 100 red tiles?

6 Explain how you can work out the number of white tiles if you know the number of red tiles.

   On the left are pieces from another mobile.

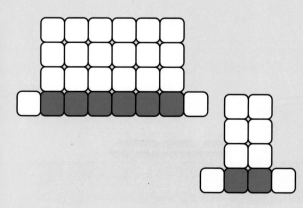

7 Without drawing, how many white tiles do you need for a piece that uses 5 red tiles?

8 How many white tiles do you need for a piece with 100 red tiles?

9 Explain how you can work out the number of white tiles if you know the number of red tiles.

25 One decimal place

This work will help you

◆ understand and use decimals

◆ put decimals in order

A Tenths

Target for the whole class or groups of three or more

One person (the teacher or one of the group) thinks of a target number.

The target should have one decimal place and be between 0 and 10.

Two other people take turns to guess the target number.

After each guess they are told if the target number is greater or less than their guess.

Target 6.3

4?

The target number is greater.

Tenths of a centimetre

This key is being measured.
Its length is 6 cm and **4 tenths** of a cm.

We write this as **6.4** cm.

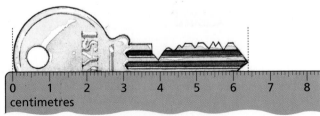

A1 Write down the length of each key, in cm.

(a)

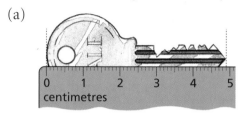

(b)

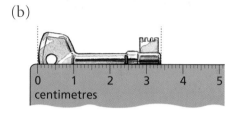

A2 Measure the length of each of these keys, in cm.

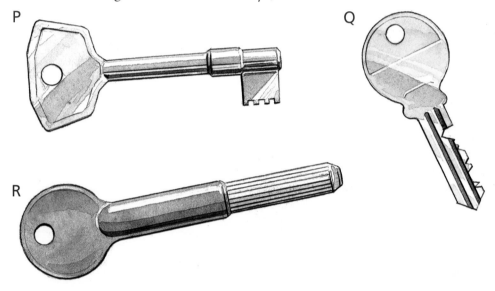

A3 (a) Which key in question A2 is the shortest?

(b) Which is the longest?

A4 Measure these keys and write them in order of length, shortest first.

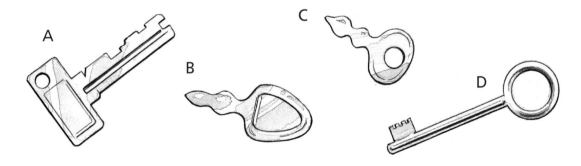

Optical illusions

A5 Which line looks longer, *a* or *b*?

Measure both lines in centimetres to see if you were right.

Write down the lengths in cm.

a

b

A6 Which line looks longer, the red line or the blue line?

Measure both lines and write down their lengths in cm.

Were you right?

A7 Which of the two thick lines looks longer, *x* or *y*?

Measure them to see if you were right.

If one line is longer, how much longer is it, in cm?

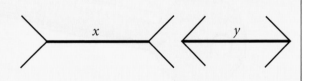

A8 Which line looks longest, *p*, *q* or *r*?

Write down the lengths in cm.

Were you right?

p

q

r

Creepy crawlies

This ladybird is only 7 tenths of
a centimetre long.

We write this as **0.7** cm.

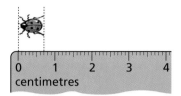

A9 Measure the length of each bug.

   (a)   (b)   (c)

A10 This is a full-size picture of a caterpillar.

   (a) Estimate its length in cm.

   (b) Measure the caterpillar and write down the length.
       How close was your estimate?

A11 Look at these full-size pictures of worms.
     Which looks longest? Which looks shortest?

   (a)   (b)

   (c)   (d)

     Measure the worms to see if you were right.
     Write down the lengths of the longest and shortest.

A12 These bees are drawn full-size.

     Which wing span looks largest?
     Which wing span looks smallest?

     Measure the wing spans to see
     if you were right.

     Write down the lengths of
     the largest and smallest.

B Reading scales to one decimal place

T

Counting on a game for two players

You will need a dice.

- Roll the dice to decide where to start on the scale below.
  If the score is 1 start at 0.1, if the score is 2 start at 0.2 and so on …

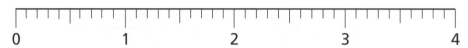

- Roll the dice again to decide the 'step' you go up every time.
  If the score is 1 the step is 0.1 each time, and so on as before.
  From your start, keep adding on your step until you run out of scale.

- List the numbers you stop at after each step.

- You win the game if you stop on 4 exactly.

Play the game a few times.
Make a table of results like this.

Start	Step	Win or lose
0.3	0.2	

Counting down   another game for two players

Use the same scale as 'Counting on'.

- This time each player decides on a point to start at between 3 and 4.
- Roll a dice to decide the step you go **down** each time.
  List the numbers the pointer stops at after each step.
- You win if you finish exactly on 0.

Make a table of starts and steps and whether they win or lose.

B1 Which number is each arrow pointing to?

(a)   (b)

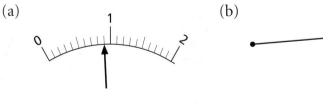

B2 Gary says that this arrow is pointing to 3.1.
Debbie says it must be 3.5, because
it's halfway between 3 and 4.

Who is right?

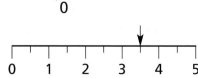

B3 Which number is each arrow pointing to?

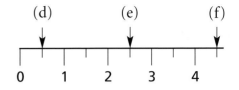

B4 Answer this on sheet 40.

B5 Copy this scale on to squared paper.
Fill in the missing numbers on the scale.

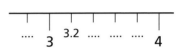

B6 Which number is each arrow pointing to?

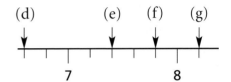

C Ordering decimals to one decimal place

C1 The lengths of five caterpillars are: 4.3 cm, 0.8 cm, 5 cm, 1.7 cm, 5.6 cm.
Write these lengths in order, shortest first.

C2 Write these lists in order of size, smallest first.

(a) 3.4, 2.8, 1.5, 0.7, 4   (b) 0.4, 2, 0.1, 4.5, 2.9
(c) 7.6, 6, 7, 8, 0.9, 1   (d) 0.7, 1.5, 1.2, 2, 0.8

C3 Here are the results of
a long jump competition.
Put the competitors in order
1st (longest jump) to 5th.

Price	6.4 m
Jamal	6.8 m
Kent	7 m
O'Brien	6.1 m
Stone	6 m

C4 In another competition, each competitor jumped twice.
Their best jump counts.

(a) What was Bryson's best jump?

	1st jump	2nd jump
Bryson	5.7 m	6 m

(b) Put these three competitors in order.

	1st jump	2nd jump
Perry	5.8 m	6 m
Davis	6.3 m	5.7 m
Conrad	6 m	6.2 m

Getting in order   a game for two players

You need cards made from sheet 41.

- Draw a board like this, with space for 8 cards.

- Deal 4 cards each.
  Don't look at your cards!

- First player: look at your first card.
  Put it on the board.

- Second player: play your first card.
  If it's **less** than the number on the board, it
  must go somewhere to the **left** of it.
  If it's **greater**, it must go somewhere to the **right**.

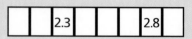

- Every time a card is played, the numbers on the
  board must be in order of size, from left to right.
  If a card won't fit, you keep it.

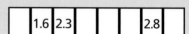

- The winner is the first player with no cards left, or
  the player with fewer cards when nobody can go.

What progress have you made?

Statement	Evidence
I can measure in tenths of a centimetre.	1 Measure the left-hand edge of this page, in centimetres.
I can read scales, to one decimal place.	2 What numbers do these arrows point to?

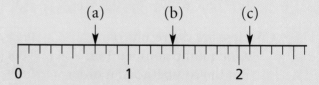

I can order decimals, to one decimal place.

3 Put these numbers in order of size, smallest first.

4.3, 0.7, 5, 1.9, 2.2

I can count on and down using decimals.

4 Copy and complete.

(a) 0.2, 0.4, 0.6, 0.8, ..., ...

(b) 0.5, 0.8, 1.1, 1.4, ..., ...

(c) 5, 4.7, 4.4, 4.1, ..., ...

(d) 3.7, 3.2, 2.7, 2.2, ..., ...

Review 3

Do not use a calculator in this review.

1 (a) Find three pairs of lines in this diagram which are perpendicular.

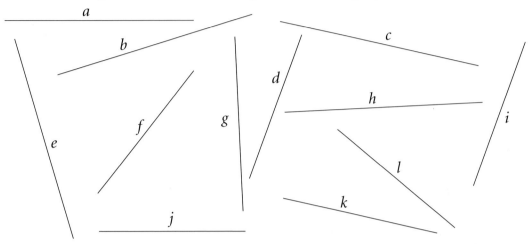

(b) Find three pairs of lines in this diagram which are parallel.

2 Here is a sketch of a shape.
Draw it accurately on plain paper.

You can use the corner of a piece of
paper to draw the right angles.

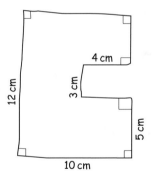

3 Draw a right-angled triangle 9 cm long and
5 cm high on plain paper.

Draw four lines, 1 cm apart, parallel to the base.

Draw a line from the top point to the middle
of the base.
Colour the pattern as shown here.

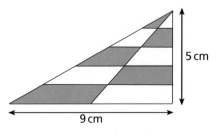

4 Work these out.

(a) 24 ÷ 6   (b) 18 ÷ 3   (c) 40 ÷ 5   (d) 21 ÷ 3   (e) 36 ÷ 6

5 Copy and complete.

(a) 32 ÷ ... = 8   (b) 42 ÷ ... = 7   (c) ... ÷ 5 = 7   (d) ... ÷ 8 = 8

6 (a) James has 32 rabbits. They sleep in hutches, 4 in each hutch.
How many hutches are needed for the rabbits?

(b) Mary's bloodhound eats three tins of dogfood each day.
How long will 18 tins of food last?

(c) Fred is packing eggs into boxes. Each box holds 6 eggs.
How many boxes are needed for 30 eggs?

7 Work these out.

(a) 11 ÷ 2   (b) 20 ÷ 3   (c) 30 ÷ 4   (d) 50 ÷ 6   (e) 60 ÷ 9

8 (a) 40 oranges are shared equally between 7 rugby players.
How many oranges do they get each? How many are left over?

(b) 49 cakes are packed into boxes. Each box holds 8 cakes.
How many boxes can be filled? How many cakes are left over?

(c) 8 greedy children share 50 bars of chocolate.
How many whole bars do they get each? How many bars are left to share out?

9 Work these out.

(a) 72 ÷ 2   (b) 123 ÷ 3   (c) 128 ÷ 4   (d) 158 ÷ 5   (e) 260 ÷ 6

10 Work out each of these. Think carefully about remainders.

(a) Paul needs to buy 130 floor tiles. They come in boxes of 8.
How many boxes does he need to buy?

(b) At a party, pensioners sit at tables for 4.
139 pensioners are coming to the party. How many tables are needed?

(c) Joy is making wooden lorries. Each lorry needs 6 wheels.
Joy has 100 wheels. How many lorries can she make?

11 We can write 'half past eight in the evening' as 8:30 p.m.
Write these times using a.m. or p.m.

(a) half past 8 in the morning   (b) a quarter past 2 in the morning

(c) a quarter to 6 in the morning   (d) a quarter to 10 at night

(e) 20 minutes to 11 at night   (f) 25 to 7 in the morning

12 Write the time that each of these clocks shows using the 24-hour clock.

(a)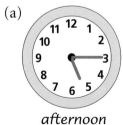

afternoon

(b)

night

(c)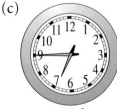

morning

(d)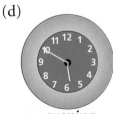

evening

158

13 Miguel is a gardener at Wrotton College. He gets to work at a quarter to 9.

(a) Miguel is asked to mow the front lawn of the college.
He starts mowing at 5 past 9.
How long is that after he gets to work?

(b) Miguel finishes mowing the lawn at 10 minutes to 11.
How long does it take him to mow the lawn?

(c) Miguel's tea-break is from 10 minutes to 11 until quarter past 11.
How many minutes does he get for his tea-break?

(d) Miguel starts weeding the front borders at a quarter past 11.
It takes him an hour and a quarter to weed the borders.
At what time does he finish?

14 Here are some tile patterns.

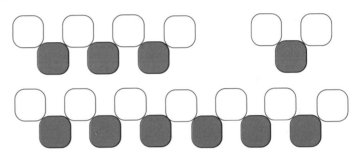

(a) Draw the pattern that has 4 red tiles.
How many white tiles does it have?

(b) Copy and complete this table.

Number of red tiles	1	2	3	4	5	6	7
Number of white tiles			4				

(c) How many white tiles would you need for a pattern with

(i) 10 red tiles   (ii) 50 red tiles

(d) Explain how you worked out your answers to (c).

(e) How can you work out the number of white tiles
if you know the number of red tiles?

15 What number does each arrow point to?

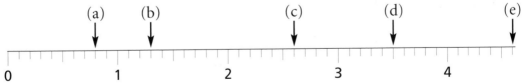

16 Write each list in order of size, smallest first.

(a) 5, 4.9, 0.9, 8, 1.1   (b) 10, 8.7, 9.1, 9.9, 7.5

(c) 0.8, 1, 0.7, 1.1, 0.2   (d) 3.5, 3, 6, 2.9, 5.5

26 Number patterns

This work will help you

◆ investigate number patterns

◆ understand prime numbers, square numbers, cubes and square roots

A Exploring a number grid

This activity is described in the teacher's guide.

The grid is on sheet 96.

A	B	C	D	E	F
1	2	3	4	5	6
7	8	9	10	11	12
13	14	15	16	17	18
19	20	21	22	23	24
25	26	27	28	29	30
31	32	33	34	35	36
37	38	39	40	41	42
43	44	45	46	47	48

1

Pick a number in column A and a number in column B.
Add your numbers together.
Which column is the result in?
Is this always true?

Investigate further.

2

Investigate the patterns made by multiples of 2, multiples of 3, and so on, in the grid.

3

Suppose the grid is extended downwards.
Can you predict the 30th number in column B?

How do you do it? Explain how to predict other numbers.

4

Can you predict which column 75 will be in?
What's the rule for predicting which column a number will be in?

B Dice numbers

You need a dice.

B1 (a) Put a dice on the table, with 5 on top.
Can you say what number is on the bottom?
Check to see if you are right.

(b) If 3 is on top, what is on the bottom?

(c) What is the rule for top and bottom numbers?

B2 For each of these dice,
add up the numbers you can see,
then add up the numbers you can't see.

(a)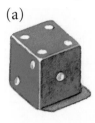

Can see 2 + 4 + 1 = 7
Can't see .....

(b)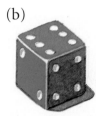

(c)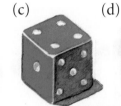

(d)

B3 (a) Can you hold a dice and see three
numbers which add up to 11?

(b) What other totals can you make like this?

(c) What is the largest total you can make?

(d) Can you make a total of 13?

*I can see 3, 5 and 1.
The total is 9.*

B4 Can you work out the total of **all** the numbers you can't
see in the pictures?

(a)

(b)

(c)

(d)

C Magic squares

This is a magic square.

If you add up each **row**
or each **column**
or each **diagonal**
you get the same total.

It is the 'magic total'.

2	9	4
7	5	3
6	1	8

C1 What is the magic total of the square above?

C2 Copy and complete these magic squares.

(a)

8	6	4
	10	5

What is the magic total of this one?

(b)

6	11	4
10		

(c)

10		6
	7	
		4

C3 (a) Look at the magic square at the top of the page.
Add 5 to every number in it and make a new square.

(b) Is the new square also a magic square?
If so, can you explain why?

7	14	

C4 Copy and complete these magic squares.
Find the magic total first!

(a)

16	3	2	13
			8
9		7	
4	15		1

(b)

15		3	
	5		
14	11	2	
1		13	12

162

D RECTANGLES

24 dots can be made into a 2 by 12 rectangle pattern.
2 and 12 are a **pair of factors** of 24
because $2 \times 12 = 24$.

2×12

Another pair of factors of 24 is 4 and 6
because $4 \times 6 = 24$.

4×6

D1 (a) Draw another rectangle pattern with 24 dots.

(b) Write down another pair of factors of 24.

D2 Here is one way to make a rectangle with 20 dots.
It shows that a pair of factors of 20 is 4 and 5
because $4 \times 5 = 20$.

4×5

Find another pair of factors of 20.

D3 Find as many ways as you can to make a rectangle pattern with

(a) 12   (b) 16 (A square counts as a rectangle.)

(c) 18   (d) 30

D4 Can you make a rectangle pattern with 17?
Are there any other numbers like 17? Give an example.

A number which can only make a single line pattern is
called a **prime** number.

2, 3, 5 and 7 are examples of prime numbers.

(1 is not a prime number. It won't even make a line.)

7 is a prime number.

It won't make a rectangle, only a line.

D5 What are the next three prime numbers after 2, 3, 5 and 7?

D6 Why is it that all prime numbers except 2 are odd numbers?

D7 One number in each of these groups is prime. Which is it?

(a) 8, 9, 10, 11, 12   (b) 14, 15, 16, 17, 18   (c) 18, 19, 20, 21, 22

(d) 22, 23, 24, 25, 26   (e) 26, 27, 28, 29, 30   (f) 31, 32, 33, 34, 35

(g) 36, 37, 38, 39, 40

E

S Q U A R E
S Q U A R E
S Q U A R E
S Q U A R E
S Q U A R E
S Q U A R E **numbers**

Numbers which can make a square pattern are called **square numbers**.

4 is a square number.   So is **16**.

E1 What are the next two square numbers in this table?

1×1	2×2	3×3	4×4	5×5	?	?
1	4	9	16	25	?	?

E2 Continue the list of square numbers up to 100.

E3 Investigate the difference between each square number and the next.
(For example, the difference between 1 and 4 is 3.)
Is there a pattern?

Multiplying a number by itself is called **squaring**.

3×3 is called **3 squared**.
It is written 3^2 (say '3 squared').

E4 Work these out.   (a) 4^2 (b) 5^2 (c) 8^2 (d) 11^2

E5 Rob thinks that 10^2 is 20. What has he done wrong?
Explain what he should have done.

E6 Work these out.   (a) 20^2 (b) 30^2 (c) 50^2 (d) 80^2

E7 Work these out.
(a) $2^2 + 3^2$ (b) $7^2 - 4^2$ (c) $8^2 + 3^2$ (d) $6^2 + 5^2$ (e) $5^2 + 7^2 + 9^2$

*E8 Write each number from 1 to 30 as the sum of square numbers
(as few as possible!).

$1 = 1^2$ $2 = 1^2 + 1^2$ $3 = 1^2 + 1^2 + 1^2$ $4 = 2^2$ $5 = 2^2 + 1^2$ ...

164

F MISS NG NUMB RS

Counting on you

4	10	16	…	…	…	…	…
5	8	11	…	…	…	…	…
60	54	48	…	…	…	…	…
88	83	78	…	…	…	…	…
100	125	150	…	…	…	…	…
1000	950	900	…	…	…	…	…

F1 (a) What are the next two numbers? **2, 5, 8, 11, 14, …, …**

(b) How did you work them out?

F2 Work out the next two numbers.
Write down the rule for working them out.

(a) **1, 8, 15, 22, 29, …, …**   (b) **31, 27, 23, 19, 15, …, …**

(c) **1, 12, 23, 34, 45, …, …**   (d) **63, 56, 49, 42, 35, …, …**

F3 Work out the missing numbers.

(a) **2, 8, 14, …, 26, …, 38**   (b) **5, 9, …, …, 21, …, 29**

(c) **…, 11, 20, …, 38, 47, …**   (d) **36, 31, …, …, 16, 11, …**

F4 One card is missing here.
What number is missing?

| 3 | 7 | 11 | 19 | 23 | 27 | 31 |

F5 Can you work out the missing numbers here?

(a) **…, …, 20, 23, …, …, 32**   (b) **…, …, 38, 30, …, 14, …**

F6 Two cards are missing here.
What numbers are missing?

| 2 | 11 | 20 | 38 | 56 | 65 | 74 |

F7 Work out the missing numbers.

(a) **7, …, 13, …, 19, …, 25**   (b) **1, …, 9, …, …, 21, …**

What progress have you made?

Statement	Evidence

I can investigate number patterns.

1

1	4	7	10	13	16	19	22
2	5	8	11	14	17	20	23
3	6	9	12	15	18	21	24

Choose a number in the second row and double it. Which row is the result in? Investigate doubling other numbers.

I know about pairs of factors and rectangle patterns.

2 (a) Draw a rectangle pattern with 10 dots.

(b) Use your pattern to write down a pair of factors of 10.

3 Write down two different pairs of factors of 36.

I know what a prime number is.

4 (a) Explain why 13 is a prime number.

(b) Write down all the prime numbers between 20 and 30.

I know about square numbers.

5 (a) Explain why 25 is a square number.

(b) What is the square of 4?

(c) Which square number is between 30 and 40?

6 Work these out.

(a) 9^2 (b) 12^2 (c) 40^2

I can continue number patterns.

7 Work out the missing numbers. Write down the rule for working them out.

(a) 5, 9, 13, 17, 21, …, …

(b) 43, 37, 31, 25, 19, …, …

(c) …, …, 24, 31, 38, 45, …

27 Rectangles

This work will help you

◆ understand the properties of rectangles

◆ translate shapes on a coordinate grid

A Properties

On the grid

This rectangle has been drawn on a 3 cm by 3 cm grid.
The rectangle is a 1 by 2 rectangle.

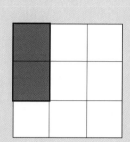

- What other different sizes of rectangle
  can you draw on this grid?
  (A square is also a rectangle!)

- How many can you draw on a 4 cm by 4 cm grid?

Answer these questions about rectangle ABCD.

A1 (a) Measure the length of side AB.

   (b) Measure the length of side AD.

A2 What type of angle is the angle at A?

A3 (a) Measure the length of diagonal AC.

   (b) Measure the length of diagonal BD.

A4 Use 'perpendicular' or 'parallel' to complete these statements.

   (a) *Side AB is* .... *to side BC.*   (b) *Side AD is* .... *to side BC.*

   (c) *Side AB is* .... *to side DC.*

A5 Draw a rectangle PQRS on squared paper, where PQ is 4 cm long
   and QR is 5 cm long.

A6 Write 'True' or 'False' for these statements about the rectangle you drew for
   question A5.

   (a) Side PQ is perpendicular to side RS.

   (b) All the angles of the rectangle are right angles.

   (c) The lengths of diagonals PR and QS are equal.

   (d) Diagonal QS is a line of symmetry of the rectangle.

   (e) Rectangle PQRS has two lines of symmetry.

B Using coordinates

B1 This is a rectangle drawn on a coordinate grid.
Write down the coordinates of these points.

(a) E   (b) F   (c) G   (d) H

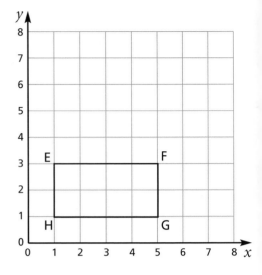

B2 Copy the grid and rectangle on to squared paper.
Draw all the lines of symmetry of the rectangle
on your diagram.

B3 The rectangle is moved 2 squares across to
the right and 3 squares up.

(a) Draw the new position of the rectangle
on your diagram.

(b) What are the new coordinates of each of the
points E, F, G and H?

> When every point in a shape is moved the same number of squares across
> and up or down a grid this is called a **translation**.

B4 (a) Draw a new grid the same size as above.

These are the coordinates of the corners of a rectangle.
Mark them on your grid and draw the rectangle.

K (4, 0)   L (7, 0)   M (7, 4)   N (4, 4)

(b) Draw the diagonals of the rectangle on your diagram.
Mark the point P where the diagonals cross.
What are the coordinates of P?

(c) Translate the rectangle 4 squares across to the left and 2 squares up.
Write down the coordinates of the corners after the translation.

What progress have you made?

Statement	Evidence
I know the properties of a rectangle.	1 (a) How many lines of symmetry does a rectangle have? (b) What angles does a rectangle always have?
I can carry out translations.	2 Write down the new coordinates of E, F, G and H above after a translation of 1 across to the left and 4 up.

28 Oral questions: measures

This work will help you

◆ find information from a table

◆ answer spoken questions

diameter

Tenpin bowling

Here is some information about the balls used in different sports.

Game	Diameter (cm)	Weight (g)	Cost (£)
Bowls (bowl)	11.7–13.3	1590	£100 for 4
Bowls (jack)	6.3–6.4	227–283	£12
Cricket	7.1–7.3	155–163	£7.50
Football	21.8–22.6	396–453	£7.50–£30
Golf	4.3	45.9	£1.30
Netball	21	400–450	£9
Pool	5.7	156–170	£30 (set of 15)
Rounders	5.4–6.0	70–85	£4
Shot (men)	11–13	7260	£10
Shot (women)	9.5–11	4000	£10
Table tennis	3.8	2.5	£3.00 for 6
Tenpin bowling	21.6	7258	£80 for a pair
Tennis	6.8	56.7–58.5	£3.90 for 3

Cricket

Golf

Tennis

Netball

Pool

Shot put

Bowls

Table tennis

Football

Rounders

169

29 Calculating with decimals

This work will help you

◆ add and subtract numbers with one decimal place

◆ multiply them by a whole number   ◆ multiply and divide by 10

A Adding and subtracting

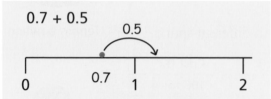

0.7 + 0.5

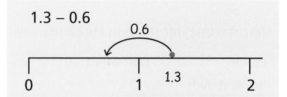

1.3 − 0.6

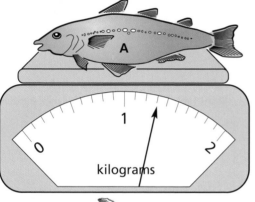

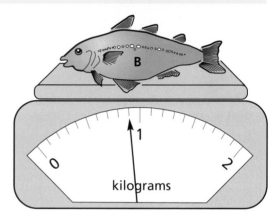

Cat	Rabbit	Guinea pig	Gerbil	Hamster
2.4 kg	1.6 kg	0.9 kg	0.6 kg	0.4 kg

One or two   a game for two players

Put the cards face up on the table.
Take turns to pick up a card.

The winner is the first person to have in their hand
three cards which add up to 1 or 2. They get one point.

The first person to win 10 points wins the whole game.

0.8   0.5   0.6   0.1
0.4   0.2   0.7   0.9
0.3

Do questions A1 to A7 in your head.

A1 (a) 0.7 + 0.4   (b) 0.3 + 0.8   (c) 0.8 + 0.9   (d) 1.2 + 0.7   (e) 1.5 + 3

A2 (a) 2.8 + 0.1   (b) 2.5 + 3.4   (c) 3.8 + 5   (d) 2.3 + 4.4   (e) 3 + 3.8

A3 (a) 1.8 + 1.6   (b) 2.6 + 0.5   (c) 1.9 + 1.7   (d) 2.9 + 0.9   (e) 3.8 + 1.7

A4 (a) 1 − 0.7   (b) 2 − 0.3   (c) 0.8 − 0.5   (d) 5 − 0.5   (e) 3 − 0.1

A5 (a) 3 − 1.5   (b) 6 − 2.3   (c) 2.8 − 1.5   (d) 3.7 − 2.4   (e) 2.8 − 2.2

A6 (a) 2.1 − 1.8   (b) 3.2 − 1.9   (c) 6.4 − 2.8   (d) 5.5 − 2.7   (e) 6.1 − 2.3

A7 (a) 1.9 + 1.5   (b) 1.9 − 1.5   (c) 2.8 + 0.7   (d) 9 − 1.8   (e) 3.6 + 3.6

A8 (a) Sam and Mel both worked out
8.3 + 5 on paper.
Who was right?

Sam	8.3	Mel	8.3
+	5		+ 5.0
	8.8		13.3

(b) Sam and Mel both worked out
8.6 + 4.5 on paper.
Who was right?

Sam	8.6	Mel	8.6
+	4.5		+ 4.5
	13.1		12.11
	1		

Do the questions below either in your head or on paper.

A9

Marrow
3.8 kg

Swede
5.4 kg

Pumpkin
8.0 kg

(a) How much do the swede and the pumpkin weigh together?
(b) How much do the marrow and the swede weigh together?
(c) How much more does the swede weigh than the marrow?
(d) How much more does the pumpkin weigh than the swede?
(e) How much more does the pumpkin weigh than the marrow?

A10 (a) 4.6 + 8.2   (b) 4.7 + 5.6   (c) 7.3 + 0.9   (d) 7 + 4.5   (e) 8.4 + 6

A11 (a) 4.5 − 1.2   (b) 6.3 − 1.8   (c) 8.4 − 3   (d) 9 − 3.7   (e) 13 − 7.2

A12 (a) 3.1 − 0.2   (b) 4.5 + 1.5   (c) 7.3 + 3   (d) 6.1 − 2.3   (e) 20 − 4.5

B Problems

B1 The body of Sam's stick insect is 7.2 cm long.
The body of Jane's stick insect is 5.5 cm long.
How much longer is Sam's stick insect than Jane's?

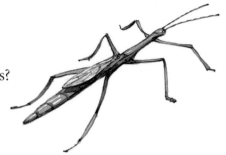

B2 Sasha goes to town and comes home a different way.
She travels 4.9 km there and 6.7 km back.
What distance does she travel altogether?

B3 Patsy is painting a fence which is 12 metres long.
So far she has painted 7.3 metres.
How much is left?

B4 A train is 4.6 metres high.
It goes under a bridge which is 5.2 metres high.
What is the size of the gap between the top of the train
and the bridge?

B5 Stan has 3 litres of water in a jug.
He fills up a bottle which holds 1.2 litres.
How much water is left in the jug?

B6 Dilesh is on a sponsored walk 12 km long.
So far he has walked 8.7 km.
How much further has he got to go?

B7 Pat has three puppies. They weigh 2.3 kg, 2.7 kg and 1.4 kg.
How much do they weigh altogether?

B8 Make up two problems in words involving decimals.
Make one an 'add' problem and the other a 'subtract' problem.
Give them to someone to do.
Don't tell them which is the 'add' and which the 'subtract'.

C Multiplying by a whole number

You know that $4 \times 3 = 12$.

This diagram shows that $\mathbf{0.4 \times 3 = 1.2}$.

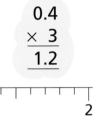

$$\begin{array}{r} 0.4 \\ \times\ 3 \\ \hline 1.2 \end{array}$$

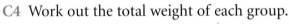

Do these questions without a calculator.

C1 Work these out.

    (a) 0.4×2 (b) 0.6×2 (c) 0.5×3

    (d) 0.8×2 (e) 0.5×4 (f) 0.4×6

C2 How many litres do these bottles hold altogether?

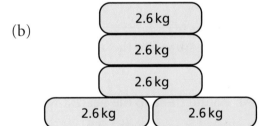

C3 Work these out.

    (a) 1.6×6 (b) 4.3×7 (c) 2.8×6

    (d) 0.6×7 (e) 2.4×9 (f) 3.7×8

C4 Work out the total weight of each group.

    (a)

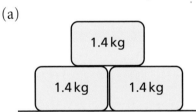

    (b)

2.6 kg
2.6 kg
2.6 kg
2.6 kg   2.6 kg

    (c)

    (d)

C5 Tina wants to make 8 curtains.
    She needs 2.6 metres of material for each curtain.
    How much material does she need altogether?

*C6 Asad's truck can carry up to 200 kg.
    He has 7 boxes, each weighing 28.4 kg.
    Can the truck carry all the boxes? Show your working.

D Rounding

3.4 is between **3** and **4**.
It is nearer to **3** than to **4**.

When we round **3.4** to the **nearest whole number** we get **3**.

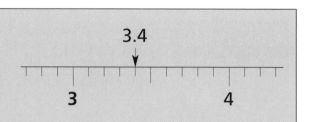

D1 What is the nearest whole number to 3.8?

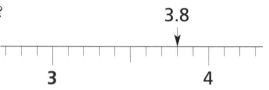

D2 Round these to the nearest whole number.

    (a) 6.9   (b) 4.7   (c) 12.2   (d) 15.8   (e) 20.4

    (f) 39.6   (g) 7.7   (h) 0.9   (i) 119.6   (j) 299.7

7.5 is exactly halfway between **7** and **8**.
So there are two 'nearest' whole numbers to **7.5**.

We usually round **up** when this happens.
So **7.5** is rounded to **8**.

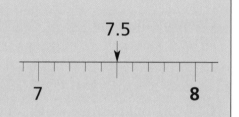

D3 Round these to the 'nearest' whole number.

    (a) 3.5   (b) 17.5   (c) 19.5   (d) 31.5   (e) 149.5

D4 Round these to the nearest whole number.

    (a) 2.7   (b) 3.9   (c) 6.4   (d) 7.5   (e) 1.8

    (f) 13.4   (g) 25.5   (h) 10.6   (i) 28.5   (j) 60.2

E Estimating by rounding

You can estimate the answer to a calculation by rounding the numbers.

Addition

$$8.7 + 3.1 + 3.9 + 7.7$$

That's roughly $9 + 3 + 4 + 8 = 24$

For each question in this section…

- Estimate the answer first, by rounding.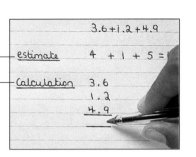
- Do the calculation.
- Compare the result with your estimate and see how close together they were.

E1 (a) 3.6 + 1.2 + 4.9   (b) 5.8 + 2.1 + 1.3

    (c) 1.8 + 3.6 + 6   (d) 4.4 + 6.7 + 1.2

E2 (a) 2.7 + 4.2 + 9.3 + 5.8   (b) 1.7 + 4.5 + 6.2 + 8.4

E3 (a) 4.2 + 3 + 6.9 + 0.7   (b) 8 + 5.8 + 0.7 + 6.1

E4 Josie did this calculation: 9.7 + 4.1 + 5 + 3.8 + 0.7.
She said that the answer was 18.8 .

How can you tell that she was wrong?

Subtraction   16.3 − 7.8

Rough estimate   16 − 8 = 8

E5 (a) 13.8 − 5.7   (b) 18.2 − 7.9   (c) 12.1 − 6.6   (d) 19 − 10.9

E6 (a) 14.4 − 6.7   (b) 17 − 13.8   (c) 14 − 2.6   (d) 9.8 − 1.9

Multiplication   8.9 × 4

Rough estimate   9 × 4 = 36

E7 (a) 2.9 × 3   (b) 5.9 × 2   (c) 6.8 × 4

E8 (a) 3.8 × 6   (b) 6.1 × 5   (c) 4.2 × 6

E9 Sue wants to make 6 shelves. Each shelf is 1.9 m long.

    (a) **Roughly** what length of wood does she need altogether?

    (b) Work out **exactly** what length of wood she needs.

F Place value

thousands hundreds tens units tenths

1 6 4 5 . 3

Do these questions without a calculator.

F1 The figure **3** in the number **1645.3** stands for **3 tenths**, or **0.3**.
What do these figures stand for?

    (a) the **1**   (b) the **6**   (c) the **4**   (d) the **5**

F2 What do these figures stand for?

    (a) the **4** in **647.8**   (b) the **9** in **203.9**   (c) the **2** in **217.5**

F3 Do these in your head.

    (a) Add 1 to 45.6   (b) Add 10 to 45.6   (c) Add 0.1 to 45.6

    (d) Add 0.1 to 135.7   (e) Add 1 to 135.7   (f) Add 10 to 135.7

F4 Do these in your head.

    (a) 32.8 + 1   (b) 32.8 + 10   (c) 32.8 + 0.1

    (d) 137.4 + 10   (e) 137.4 + 0.1   (f) 137.4 + 1

F5   Pam started with this number.   **356.4**
She subtracted a number and the result was   **306.4**
    What number did she subtract?

F6   Dan started with this number.   **497.6**
He subtracted a number and the result was   **490.6**
    What number did he subtract?

F7   Rob started with this number.   **685.7**
He subtracted a number and the result was   **685.0**
    What number did he subtract?

F8 We can write $4\frac{3}{10}$ as the decimal 4.3.
Write each of these as decimals.

    (a) $6\frac{7}{10}$ (b) $1\frac{3}{10}$ (c) $2\frac{1}{10}$ (d) $10\frac{9}{10}$ (e) $\frac{6}{10}$

F9 Write each of these using fractions.

    (a) 2.9   (b) 7.3   (c) 8.1   (d) 0.3

G Multiplying and dividing by 10

Multiplying by 10

- Use a calculator to multiply each of these numbers by 10.

  | 4.2 | 2.6 | 38.7 | 0.9 | 1.6 | 0.2 |

- What will you get when you multiply each of these numbers by 10?
  Check each one with a calculator.

  | 0.6 | 5.9 | 72.4 | 0.8 | 7.6 | 0.3 |

When you multiply by 10,

tens become **hundreds**

units become **tens**

tenths become **units**

So every figure moves **one place to the left**.

G1 Write down the results of these, without using a calculator.

(a) 3.4×10 (b) 0.2×10 (c) 1.4×10 (d) 2.1×10 (e) 0.3×10

(f) 10×1.7 (g) 10×5.4 (h) 10×15.1 (i) 2.7×10 (j) 10×20.4

G2 Do these without a calculator.

(a) 13.7×10 (b) 53.2×10 (c) 1.8×10 (d) 10×4.6 (e) 5.6×10

(f) 10×3.3 (g) 0.7×10 (h) 10×19.4 (i) 32.5×10 (j) 10×16.0

Dividing by 10

- Use a calculator to divide each of these numbers by 10.

  | 37 | 56 | 187 | 8 | 45 | 3 |

- What will you get when you divide each of these numbers by 10?
  Check each one with a calculator.

  | 246 | 12 | 5 | 74 | 2 | 68 |

When you divide by 10,

hundreds become **tens**

tens become **units**

units become **tenths**

So every figure moves **one place to the right**.

G3 Write down the results of these, without using a calculator.

(a) $43 \div 10$ (b) $27 \div 10$ (c) $133 \div 10$ (d) $648 \div 10$ (e) $6 \div 10$

(f) $67 \div 10$ (g) $25 \div 10$ (h) $4 \div 10$ (i) $42 \div 10$ (j) $125 \div 10$

G4 Do these without a calculator.

(a) $36 \div 10$ (b) $9 \div 10$ (c) $16 \div 10$ (d) $70 \div 10$ (e) $31 \div 10$

(f) $136 \div 10$ (g) $55 \div 10$ (h) $130 \div 10$ (i) $21 \div 10$ (j) $7 \div 10$

G5 Do these without a calculator. Some are $\times 10$ and some are $\div 10$.

(a) 4.7×10 (b) $36 \div 10$ (c) 38×10 (d) 10×0.1 (e) $268 \div 10$

(f) $157 \div 10$ (g) 38.6×10 (h) $74 \div 10$ (i) 71×10 (j) $19 \div 10$

What progress have you made?

Statement	Evidence
I can add and subtract numbers with one decimal place in my head.	1 Work these out in your head. (a) $0.9 + 0.3$ (b) $1.6 + 0.8$ (c) $3.3 + 1.9$ (d) $4 - 0.5$ (e) $7 - 2.2$ (f) $6.3 - 1.8$
I can add and subtract numbers with one decimal place without a calculator.	2 Work these out on paper or in your head. (a) $7.9 + 3.6$ (b) $8.6 - 4.8$ (c) $5.3 + 3.9$ (d) $4.2 - 3.5$ (e) $7.8 + 2.7$ (f) $6.1 - 4.9$
I can multiply tenths by a whole number.	3 Work these out. (a) 0.6×5 (b) 2.7×4
I can use rounding to help check calculations.	4 Estimate the answer to each of these. Then work out the exact answer. (a) $1.8 + 5.6 + 8.9$ (b) $14.7 - 12.9$ (c) 5.8×7 (d) $9.9 + 3.1 + 7.8$
I know what the figures stand for in a number with one decimal place.	5 What do these figures stand for? (a) the 7 in 276.4 (b) the 3 in 49.3
I can multiply and divide by 10 without a calculator.	6 Work these out without a calculator. (a) 5.6×10 (b) $362 \div 10$ (c) $231 \div 10$ (d) 10×4.3 (e) $8 \div 10$ (f) 0.7×10

 **Chance**

This is about games and other situations where the outcome is uncertain because it is a matter of chance.

The work will help you

◆ decide whether a game is fair or unfair

◆ understand the probability scale

◆ write a probability as a fraction

A Chance or skill?

Some games are games of skill. Some are games of chance.
Many games involve both chance and skill.

There are three games on sheets 111, 112 and 113.

Play each game and decide if they are games of skill or chance.
Some may involve both skill and chance.

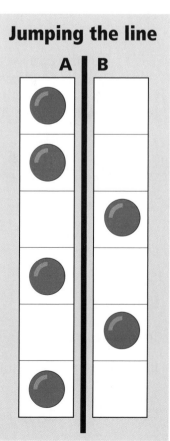

Fours

Line of three

1	3	●	4	3	3
2	●	3	2	2	2
4	2	1	1	●	6
1	●	6	6	5	3
5	5	5	4	●	5
4	4	●	1	4	6

Jumping the line

A   B

B Fair or unfair?

Three way race

For three players (A, B and C)

Each puts a counter at the start of the track.

Two dice are rolled.

If both numbers are even, A moves forward one space.

If both numbers are odd, B moves forward one space.

If one number is even and one odd, C moves forward one space.

The first to get to the end of the track is the winner.

Finish		
	Start	
A	**B**	**C**

- Play the game several times.
  Keep a record of who wins (A, B or C).

Winner	Tally	Number of wins
A	ⵜⵜⵜ I	
B	III	
C	II	

- Is it a fair game? Do A, B and C all have the same chance of winning?

Rat races

Teacher-led games

Play the two rat race games with your teacher.

Are these games fair?
Does every rat have an equal chance of winning?

C Probability

Probability is a way of saying how likely something is.

Something that has no chance of happening has probability 0.
Something that is certain to happen has probability 1.

Things that have a chance of happening have probabilities between 0 and 1.

This is a probability washing line.

Where would you hang these on the line?

- The probability that a coin lands heads
- The probability that Rat 1 wins the second rat race
- The probability that the sun will rise tomorrow morning
- The probability that a particular ticket wins the National Lottery

Make up some more examples.

C1 Use one of these words to describe each of the statements below.

| Impossible | Unlikely | A 50% chance | Likely | Certain |

If I roll an ordinary dice it will show

(a) a 6   (b) an even number   (c) a 7

(d) a number less than 10   (e) a number greater than 1

C2 Draw a probability scale like this.

$$0 \qquad\qquad\qquad \frac{1}{2} \qquad\qquad\qquad 1$$

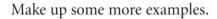

Mark these roughly on your scale with arrows.

(a) The probability that when you roll a dice you get an even number

(b) The probability that when you roll a dice you get a 6

C3 Out of every 1000 babies born, 515 are boys and 485 are girls.

(a) Is a new-born baby more likely to be a boy or a girl?

(b) On the scale you drew, mark roughly the probability that a new-born baby will be a boy.

C4 Which event below goes with each of the arrows on the probability line?

$$0 \quad\quad\quad \overset{\textbf{P}}{\downarrow} \quad\quad\quad \overset{\textbf{Q}}{\downarrow} \quad\quad \overset{\textbf{R}}{\downarrow} \quad\quad\quad\quad 1$$

(a) Choosing a heart from a shuffled pack of cards

(b) Getting 1, 2, 3 or 4 when you roll a dice

(c) Choosing a red pen from a pencil case with 5 red and 5 black pens

D Spinners

TRY YOUR LUCK!
PICK A COLOUR

Sometimes a spinner is used instead of a dice.

This spinner has five equal sections.
You spin the arrow. When it stops, it points to a colour.

The spinner is fair.
Every section has the same probability of winning.

Suppose you have chosen yellow.
The probability that yellow will win is $\frac{1}{5}$.

Two sections are coloured red.
The probability that red will win is $\frac{2}{5}$.

D1 Match the cards here with the probability that red will win on each of these spinners.

$\dfrac{1}{8}$ $\quad\dfrac{1}{6}$ $\quad\dfrac{1}{4}$ $\quad\dfrac{1}{2}$

(a)   (b)   (c)   (d)

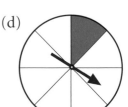

D2 Which of these fractions shows the probability that green will win on this spinner? $\dfrac{2}{3}$ $\quad\dfrac{1}{5}$ $\quad\dfrac{2}{5}$

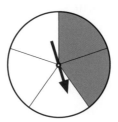

D3 What is the probability that blue will win on each of these spinners?

(a) 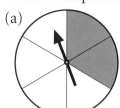   (b) 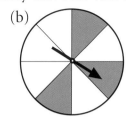   (c) 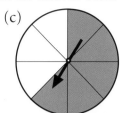   (d)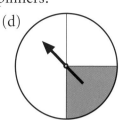

D4 With this spinner, what is the probability that

(a) yellow wins

(b) blue wins

(c) white wins

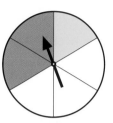

D5 With this spinner, what is the probability that

(a) red wins

(b) blue wins

(c) white wins

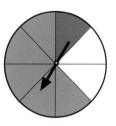

D6 With this spinner, what is the probability that red will **not** win?

D7 What is the probability that red will **not** win on each of these spinners?

(a)    (b) 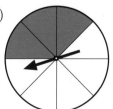   (c)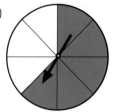

D8 What is the probability that red **will** win on each of these spinners?

(a)    (b) 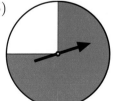   (c)

Make your own spinner

Draw a circle and divide it into equal sections.
You can colour the sections or number them.

Put a pencil or compass point through a paper clip,
so that the point is at the centre of the circle.

Spin the paper clip and see where it stops.

- How can you check if your spinner is fair?

What progress have you made?

Statement	Evidence

I can find out by experiment
whether a game of chance is fair
or unfair.

1 Find out if this game is fair.

There are two players, A and B.
They take turns to throw two dice.
If both numbers are less than 4, A wins a point.
If not, then B wins a point.

The first to get 10 points wins the game.

I understand the probability scale.

2 Which letter on this probability scale shows the
probability of each of the events below?

```
        K        L              M
0       ↓        ↓              ↓       1
├────────────────────────────────────┤
```

(a) Choosing a red card (heart or diamond)
from a pack of playing cards

(b) Choosing a red sweet from a bag with
7 red sweets and 1 yellow sweet

(c) Rolling a 5 or a 6 with a dice

I can write a probability as a fraction.

3 On this spinner, what is the probability that

(a) blue will win

(b) blue will not win

(c) red will win

(d) red will not win

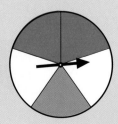

③① **Negative numbers**

This work will help you

- ◆ put negative numbers in order
- ◆ find differences between negative numbers
- ◆ use graphs and charts with negative numbers

A **Colder and colder**

Temperature is usually measured in **degrees Celsius** (°C).

Water boils at 100°C.

Room temperature is about 20°C.

Water freezes at 0°C.

The temperature inside a home freezer should be about ⁻18°C.

What kinds of thermometer have you seen?

185

For discussion

Put these temperatures in order from the highest to the lowest.

A A winter's day temperature at the North Pole

B Human body temperature

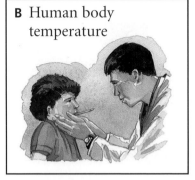

C Temperature of a hot summer's day in Britain

D Antarctic sea water temperature

E Temperature inside an ordinary fridge

F Temperature inside a car in the morning after a frosty night

G Temperature of a hot bath

H Temperature at which butter melts

I Temperature of a hot bowl of soup

J Oven temperature for baking a cake

K Temperature of ice-cream when it's good to eat

L Temperature of a heated swimming pool

186

A1 This question is on sheet 90.

A2 (a) Which of these temperatures is lowest?

-6°C   -4°C   -8°C

(b) Which of these temperatures is highest?

-10°C   -2°C   -3°C

(c) Which of these temperatures is highest?

-10°C   2°C   -6°C

(d) Which of these temperatures is lowest?

7°C   -9°C   -4°C

A3 (a) Write down the temperature in each of these cities.

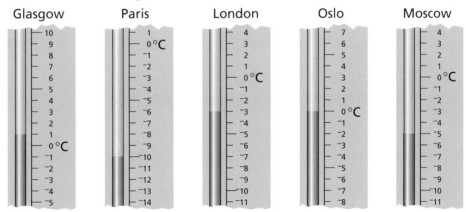

Glasgow   Paris   London   Oslo   Moscow

(b) Which city has the coldest temperature?

(c) Which city has the warmest temperature?

A4 Which is the colder temperature, -2°C or -4°C?

A5 Which of these temperatures is lowest?   -12°C, -4°C, 2°C, -8°C

A6 Write these temperatures in order, the lowest first.

7°C   -15°C   3°C   0°C   -5°C

A7 Make these statements true by using < (less than) or > (greater than)
in the spaces.

(a) 3°C … 9°C   (b) -4°C … 1°C   (c) -1°C … 3°C   (d) -2°C … -5°C

(e) -5°C … 3°C   (f) -3°C … -1°C   (g) 4°C … -5°C   (h) 0°C … -3°C

A8 Here are some thermometers.

(a) Write down the temperature shown on each one.

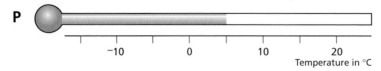

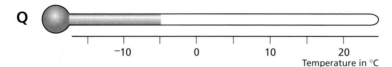

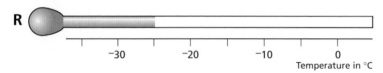

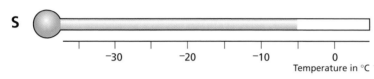

> Food which is kept cool will stay fresh longer.
> - A normal fridge should keep food between 5°C and 0°C.
> - Freezers should keep food at or below ⁻18°C.

(b) Which of the thermometers P, Q, R and S show a temperature suitable for a freezer?

A9 Say whether these are a suitable temperature for a freezer, fridge or neither.

(a) ⁻25°C   (b) 3°C   (c) ⁻15°C   (d) 1°C

A10 This is a notice on a deep freezer.

Which of these temperatures is suitable for this deep freezer?

IMPORTANT
Temperature of freezer must be ≤ ⁻20°C

(a) ⁻25°C   (b) ⁻15°C   (c) 5°C

(d) ⁻20°C   (e) ⁻18°C   (f) ⁻23°C

Temperature trumps

The cards for this game are on sheets 91 and 92.

B Temperature changes

This map shows the noon temperature at some cities in Europe on a January day.

- Which city was warmer, Berlin or Budapest?

- How many degrees warmer was Madrid than Berlin?

- Warsaw was 3 degrees warmer than Stockholm.

  What was the temperature in Warsaw?

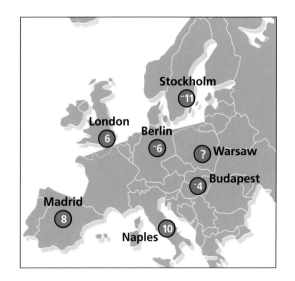

B1 What temperature is

(a) 4 degrees lower than 7°C   (b) 4 degrees lower than 3°C

(c) 5 degrees lower than 1°C   (d) 4 degrees lower than 0°C

(e) 5 degrees lower than ⁻3°C   (f) 5 degrees higher than ⁻3°C

B2 At midday the temperature was 8°C.
At midnight the temperature was ⁻5°C.
How many degrees did the temperature fall between midday and midnight?

B3 At dawn the temperature was ⁻11°C.
At midday the temperature was 4°C.
How many degrees did the temperature rise between dawn and midday?

B4 Make some true sentences by putting any of the numbers below in the spaces.

A temperature of ....°C is ...... degrees higher than a temperature of ....°C.

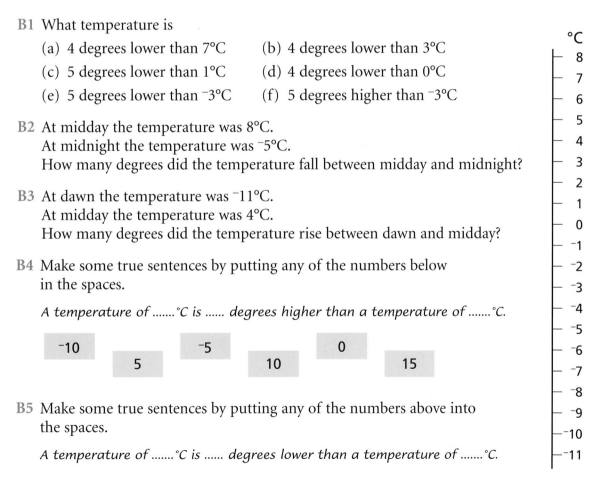

B5 Make some true sentences by putting any of the numbers above into the spaces.

A temperature of ....°C is ...... degrees lower than a temperature of ....°C.

C Using tables

C1 These are the temperatures at midnight in Helsinki for the first fortnight in May.

May	1	2	3	4	5	6	7	8	9	10	11	12	13	14
Temp. (°C)	⁻10	⁻8	⁻7	⁻8	⁻3	1	1	2	3	2	3	⁻1	⁻1	2

(a) On how many days was the midnight temperature above freezing?

(b) How many degrees difference is there between the midnight temperature on 1st May and 9th May?

C2 This table shows the temperatures at noon and midnight for a town in Canada for the first fortnight in April.

April	1	2	3	4	5	6	7	8	9	10	11	12	13	14
Noon temp. (°C)	⁻10	⁻12	⁻12	⁻6	0	0	2	3	5	⁻1	⁻2	⁻1	3	5
Midnight temp. (°C)	⁻21	⁻18	⁻19	⁻14	⁻9	⁻8	⁻5	⁻2	2	⁻5	⁻7	⁻5	⁻2	1

Which of these statements are true?

(a) For half the fortnight noon temperatures were below freezing.

(b) It was always freezing at midnight.

(c) If it was freezing at noon, it was always freezing at midnight.

(d) On April 2nd it was 6 degrees colder at midnight than at noon.

C3 This table shows the average monthly temperatures at Scott base (in Antarctica) and Nord base (in the Arctic).

Month	Jan	Feb	Mar	Apr	May	Jun	Jul	Aug	Sep	Oct	Nov	Dec
Scott (°C)	⁻20	⁻40	⁻54	⁻57	⁻58	⁻58	⁻60	⁻60	⁻58	⁻51	⁻38	⁻28
Nord (°C)	⁻30	⁻30	⁻31	⁻24	⁻11	0	4	1	⁻9	⁻18	⁻23	⁻26

(a) Which of the two bases is colder in July?

(b) Which of the two bases is warmer in August?

(c) By how many degrees is Scott base warmer than Nord base in January?

(d) For how many months in the year is the temperature at Nord base below zero?

(e) Which three months of the year do you think are summer at Nord base?

(f) Which three months are summer at Scott base?

D Temperature graphs

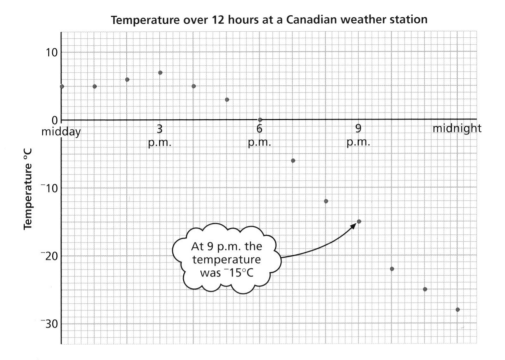

Temperature over 12 hours at a Canadian weather station

At 9 p.m. the temperature was ⁻15°C

D1 This graph shows the temperatures every hour from midday to midnight at a Canadian weather station.

(a) What was the temperature at 3 p.m.?

(b) When was the temperature ⁻12°C?

(c) What was the lowest temperature recorded?

(d) What time was the lowest temperature recorded?

(e) What was the highest temperature recorded?

(f) By how many degrees did the temperature drop between 8 p.m. and midnight?

D2 This graph shows the outdoor temperature during a night.

(a) What was the temperature at 10:30 p.m.?

(b) What was the lowest temperature?

(c) At what times was the temperature ⁻10°C?

(d) For how long was the temperature below ⁻5°C?

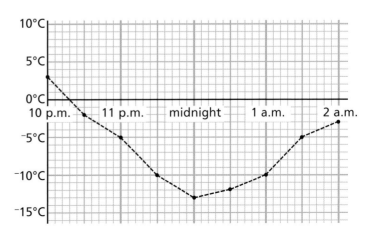

D3 This bar chart shows mean monthly temperatures at noon in Wellington.

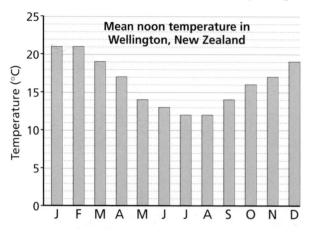

(a) In which months was the mean temperature at noon hotter than 20°C?

(b) In which months was the mean temperature at noon colder than 14°C?

(c) What is the difference in mean noon temperature between January and August?

D4 This line graph shows the mean noon and midnight temperatures in New York.

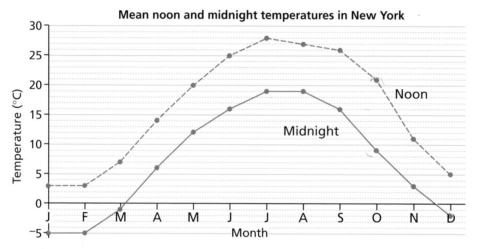

(a) What is the mean noon temperature in June?

(b) What is the mean midnight temperature in January?

(c) Which months have the lowest mean midnight temperature?

(d) What is the difference between the mean noon and midnight temperatures in March?

(e) Look at the mean temperatures in December.
How many degrees higher is the mean at noon than at midnight?

(f) Which month has the biggest difference between the mean temperatures at noon and midnight?

What progress have you made?

Statement

I can put negative numbers in order.

I can find differences between negative numbers.

I can read graphs which include negative numbers.

Evidence

1 Put these temperatures in order, lowest first.

2°C ⁻3°C ⁻32°C 15°C ⁻14°C ⁻1°C

2 These are the noon temperatures on a January day at some cities in the USA.
Boston   ⁻12°C   Chicago   ⁻7°C
Miami   21°C   Los Angeles 16°C

(a) How many degrees warmer was Los Angeles than Chicago?

(b) How many degrees warmer was Chicago than Boston?

(c) Denver was 20°C warmer than Boston. What was the temperature in Denver?

3 This graph shows the temperature in °C on a winter's night somewhere in England.

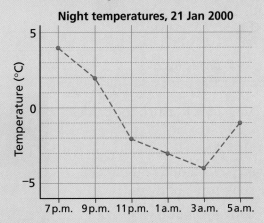

Night temperatures, 21 Jan 2000

(a) What temperature was it at 1 a.m.?

(b) How many degrees difference was there between the temperatures at 7 p.m. and 11 p.m.?

(c) Between which two times did the temperature change the most?

(d) At 7 a.m. the temperature had risen by 3 degrees from 5 a.m.
What was the temperature at 7 a.m.?

Action and result puzzles

These puzzles involve adding, subtracting, multiplying and dividing.
Doing them will help you

- ◆ carry out these sorts of calculations in your head
- ◆ understand more about what happens when you do these calculations
- ◆ explain your methods to other people and listen to their explanations

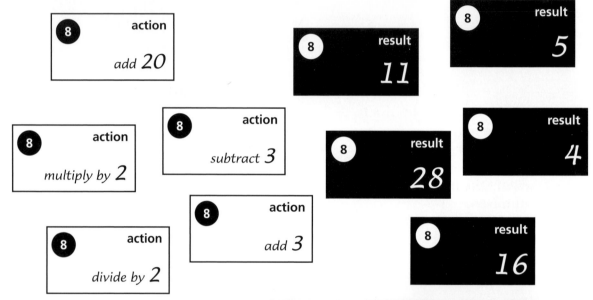

8 **action**
add 20

8 **result**
11

8 **result**
5

8 **action**
multiply by 2

8 **action**
subtract 3

8 **result**
28

8 **result**
4

8 **action**
divide by 2

8 **action**
add 3

8 **result**
16

- How do you match the cards?

There are several different puzzles.
Try to solve some of them.

Try making up your own puzzles.

Review 4

1 You can make several rectangle patterns from 36. Here is one.

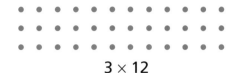

3×12

(a) Draw another rectangle pattern for 36.

(b) How many different pairs of factors can you find for 36?

(c) Is 36 a square number? Explain.

2 Work these out. (a) $4^2 - 3^2$ (b) $1^2 + 2^2 + 3^2$ (c) $10^2 - 8^2$

3 Work out. (a) 40^2 (b) 70^2 (c) $60^2 - 50^2$

4 Look at the numbers in this box.

4	6	12	24	35	36	49

(a) Are any of the numbers prime? If so, which?

(b) Are any of the numbers square? If so, which?

5 Work out the next two numbers in each of these. Write down the rule for working them out.

(a) 1, 4, 7, 10, 13, 16, ..., ...

(b) 100, 94, 88, 82, 76, 70, ..., ...

(c) 0.2, 0.7, 1.2, 1.7, 2.2, 2.7, ..., ...

(d) 11, 20, 29, 38, 47, 56, ..., ...

(e) 10, 9.7, 9.4, 9.1, 8.8, 8.5, ..., ...

6 Copy this diagram onto centimetre squared paper.

(a) What special name do we give to the shape ABCD?

(b) What is the area of shape ABCD?

(c) What is the perimeter of the shape?

(d) On your diagram, draw all the lines of symmetry of the shape.

(e) The shape is translated 1 square to the left and 2 squares down. Draw the new position of the shape.

(f) Write down the coordinates of the new positions of the points A, B, C and D.

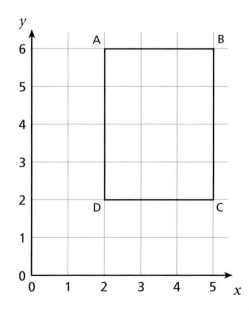

7 Without a calculator, work these out.

(a) $2.3 + 1.2$ (b) $4 - 0.6$ (c) $3.9 + 0.2$ (d) $7 - 1.2$ (e) $0.8 + 0.9$

(f) $3 - 1.8$ (g) $1.9 + 1.9$ (h) $6 - 1.4$ (i) $6.2 - 1.4$ (j) $10 - 5.5$

8 Do these without a calculator.

(a) 1.3×2 (b) 2.4×2 (c) 1.2×3 (d) 0.8×4 (e) 1.3×8

(f) 1.9×10 (g) 10×2.5 (h) 15×10 (i) 10×27.3 (j) 18.3×10

(k) $55 \div 10$ (l) $9 \div 10$ (m) $100 \div 10$ (n) $17 \div 10$ (o) $65 \div 10$

9 A double-decker bus is 4.1 metres tall.
It goes under a 5 metre high bridge.
What is the gap between the top of the bus and the bridge?

10 Cath's four kittens weigh 1.1 kg, 1.5 kg, 0.9 kg and 1.3 kg.

(a) How much do they weigh altogether?

(b) One month later, each kitten has gained 0.5 kg in weight.
How much do they weigh altogether now?

11 Cora is carrying bottles of water back from the shops.
She has 6 bottles of water and each weighs 1.5 kg.

(a) How much do the bottles weigh altogether?

(b) Balir is carrying four cans of oil. Each can weighs 1.9 kg.
Is he carrying more or less weight than Cora?
How many kilograms more or less?

12 Round each of these to the nearest whole number.

(a) 12.8 (b) 7.5 (c) 10.1 (d) 110.7 (e) 9.8

13 For each of these calculations, first estimate the answer by rounding.
Then do the exact calculation without a calculator.

(a) $3.9 + 2.9 + 7.1$ (b) $12.8 - 7.9$ (c) 0.9×6

(d) $4.1 + 3.9 + 12.9$ (e) $20 - 12.9$ (f) 2.1×8

14 Use one of these words to describe each of the statements below.

| Impossible | Unlikely | A 50% chance | Likely | Certain |

If I pick a card from an ordinary pack

(a) it will be an ace   (b) it will be a red card   (c) it will be red or black

15 Draw a line like this, about 10 cm long.
Mark 0 and 1 at the ends.

0 _____ 1

Draw and label arrows on your line to mark roughly
the probability of these.

(a) Getting a tail when you spin a coin.

(b) Rolling a number less than 6 with a dice.

(c) Picking the ace of spades from a pack of cards.

(d) In a raffle with 100 tickets, your ticket is not picked out first.

16 What is the probability that red will win on each of these spinners?

(a) 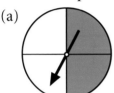 (b) 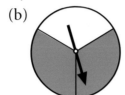 (c) 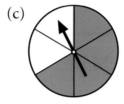 (d)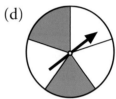

17 What is the probability that red will **not** win
for each of the spinners in question 4?

18 The map shows the temperature at
midnight in some cities in January.

(a) Which city is coldest?

(b) Which city is warmest?

(c) Which city is warmer, Oslo or Cracow?
By how many degrees?

(d) How many degrees colder is
Archangel than Cardiff?

(e) There is a difference in temperature
of 20 degrees between two cities.
Which cities are they?

(f) London is 5 degrees warmer than Lyons.
What is the temperature in London?

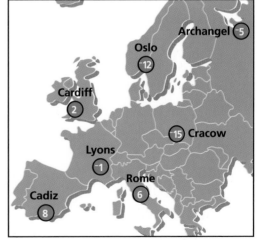

19 Write these temperatures in order, coldest first.

12°C   ⁻1°C   2°C   ⁻18°C   0°C   ⁻10°C

20 Copy and complete each of these, using either < or >.

(a) 2°C … 6°C   (b) 2°C … ⁻6°C   (c) ⁻2°C … 6°C   (d) ⁻2°C … ⁻6°C

33 Two decimal places

This work will help you

◆ understand numbers with two decimal places

◆ put decimals in order

A Tenths review

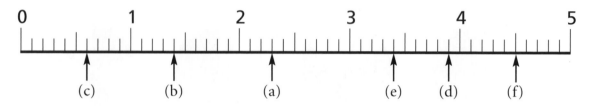

A1 What number does each arrow above point to?

A2 What number (as a decimal) is halfway between 2 and 3?

A3 Find 2.9 on the number line. What is 2.9 + 0.1?

A4 Find 1 on the number line. What is 1 − 0.1?

A5 Write these numbers in order, smallest first. 3, 4.6, 2.8, 5, 0.9

A6 Katy did 1.3 + 2 like this.   What should the answer be?

$$
\begin{array}{r}
1.3 \\
+\quad 2 \\
\hline
1.5 \\
\end{array}
$$
✗

A7 Work these out.

(a) 2.3 + 1.4   (b) 3.5 + 4.7   (c) 5 + 2.6   (d) 3.6 + 4

A8 Work these out.

(a) 5.7 − 2.3   (b) 8.5 − 2.9   (c) 7 − 1.3   (d) 6.6 − 4

A9 Do these in your head.

(a) Add 1 to 23.6   (b) Add 10 to 23.6   (c) Add 0.1 to 23.6

(d) 145.6 + 10   (e) 145.6 + 0.1   (f) 10 − 0.1

A10 What do these figures stand for?

(a) The 3 in 234.1   (b) The 7 in 431.7   (c) The 4 in 530.4

B Tenths and hundredths

This amount of water is between 7 tenths and 8 tenths of a litre.

It is **7 tenths and 4 hundredths** of a litre.

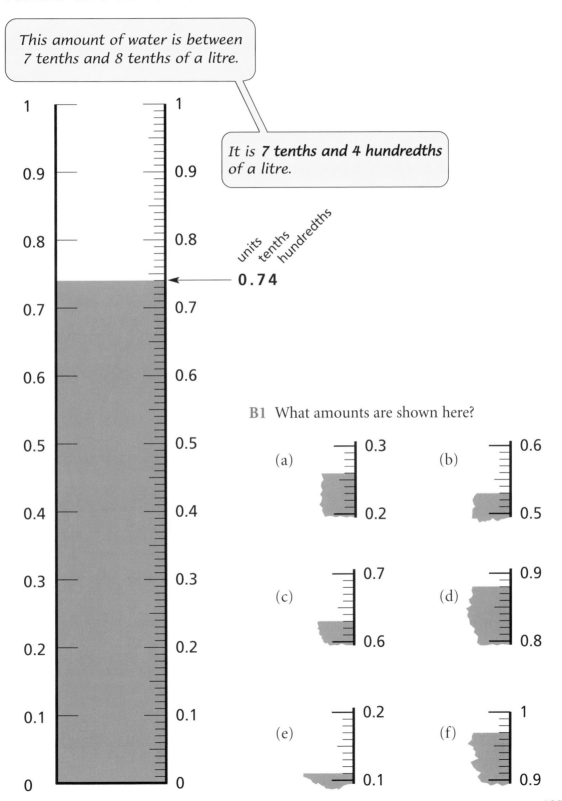

B1 What amounts are shown here?

(a)   (b)

(c)   (d)

(e)   (f)

B2 What number does each arrow point to?

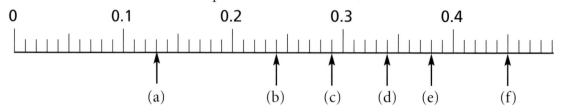

B3 (a) What number is halfway between 0.2 and 0.3?
(The diagram above may help.)

(b) What number is halfway between 0.1 and 0.2?

(c) What number is halfway between 0.3 and 0.4?

(d) What number is halfway between 0.6 and 0.7?

B4 What is the length of each of these pins, in cm?

(a)　　　　　　　　　　　　　　　　(b)

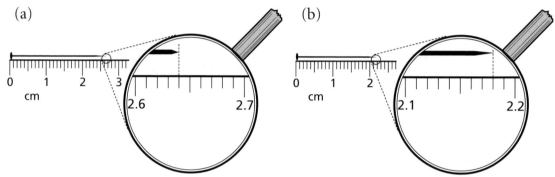

B5 What number does each arrow point to?

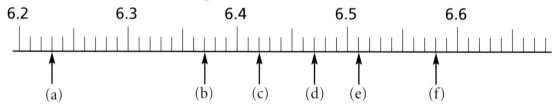

B6 (a) What number is halfway between 6.2 and 6.3?
(The diagram above may help.)

(b) What number is halfway between 6.4 and 6.5?

(c) What number is halfway between 6.5 and 6.6?

(d) What number is halfway between 6.7 and 6.8?

B7 What numbers are
marked with arrows?

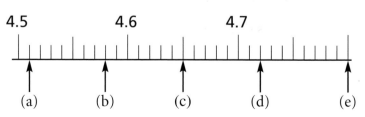

C Less than 0.1

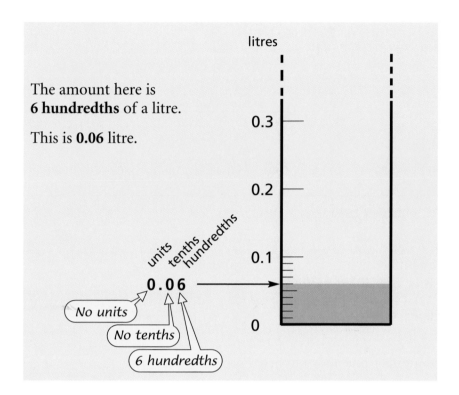

The amount here is **6 hundredths** of a litre.

This is **0.06** litre.

C1 What amounts are shown here?

(a) (b) (c) (d)

C2 What number does each arrow point to?

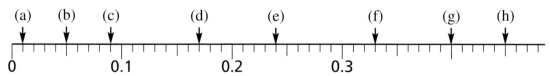

C3 This question is on sheet 223.

C4 Write these as decimals.

(a) five hundredths   (b) 9 hundredths   (c) one hundredth

D 0.3 and 0.30 are equal

The top number line is divided into **tenths**.
3 tenths, or **0.3**, is marked with an arrow.

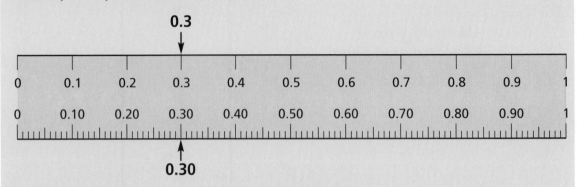

The bottom number line is divided into **hundredths**.
30 hundredths, or **0.30**, is marked with an arrow.

0.3 and **0.30** are equal.

D1 Use the number line above to help you

(a) write another decimal equal to 0.7

(b) write another decimal equal to 0.1

(c) write another decimal equal to 0.80

(d) write another decimal equal to 0.40

D2 (a) What number is halfway between 0.7 and 0.8?

(b) What number is halfway between 0.9 and 1?

(c) What number is halfway between 0 and 0.1?

D3 Find where these numbers are on the number lines above.

0.05, 0.5, 0.3

Write them in order of size, smallest first.

D4 Write each list of numbers in order of size, smallest first.
Use the number lines to help you.

(a) 0.9, 0.2, 0.65   (b) 0.4, 0.15, 0.08   (c) 0.62, 0.3, 0.07, 0.1

D5 Write these lists in order, smallest first,
without looking at the number lines.

(a) 0.6, 0.03, 0.25, 0.61   (b) 0.1, 0.06, 0.3, 0.17   (c) 0.55, 0.6, 0.08, 0.5

E Decimals of a metre

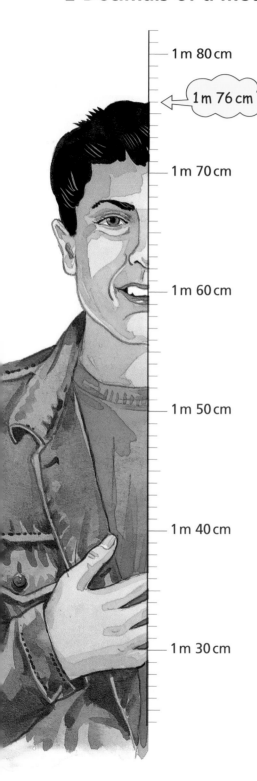

— 1 m 80 cm

1 m 76 cm

— 1 m 70 cm

— 1 m 60 cm

— 1 m 50 cm

— 1 m 40 cm

— 1 m 30 cm

A metre is divided into 100 **centimetres**.
Each centimetre is **one hundredth** of a metre.

A height of 1 metre and 76 centimetres can be written as
1.76 metres ('one point seven six metres').

- One way to write **1 metre and 30 cm**
  is 1.30 metres.

  Enter 1.30 into a calculator and press ⎡=⎤.
  It says 1.3. Why?

- Which is greater, 1.8 metres or 1.38 metres? Why?

- How do you write in decimals **1 metre and 5 cm**?

E1 Write these in metres using decimals.

(a) 3 metres and 25 centimetres

(b) 4 metres and 68 centimetres

E2 Write 139 cm in (a) metres and cm (b) metres

E3 Write these in metres.

(a) 1 metre and 70 cm (b) 1 metre and 7 cm

(c) 2 metres and 45 cm (d) 3 metres and 6 cm

E4 (a) Hitesh is 147 cm tall. Write his height in metres.

(b) Sadia is 107 cm tall. Write her height in metres.

(c) Gail is 160 cm tall. Write her height in metres.

E5 Copy and complete this table.
It shows the heights of three people.

Name	Height in cm	Height in metres and cm	Height in metres
Alan	167 cm		
Kira		1 m 8 cm	
Greg			1.4 m

E6 Here are the lengths of four snakes.

Cobra 3.05 m   Python 3.17 m   Boa constrictor 3.3 m   Mamba 3.1 m

(a) Which is the shortest snake?

(b) Which is the longest?

E7 Put these lengths in order, shortest first.

1.4 m   1.18 m   1.66 m

E8 Put these lengths in order, shortest first.

0.7 m   0.53 m   0.09 m

E9 This is part of a measuring tape.
What numbers do the arrows point to?

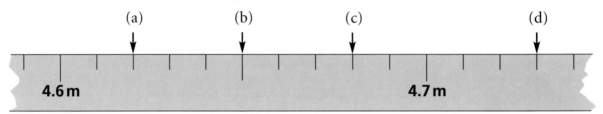

E10 What numbers do these arrows point to?

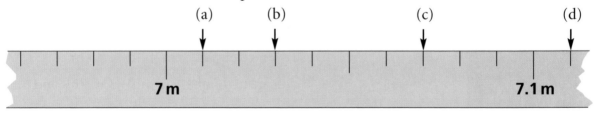

E11 This question is on sheet 224.

Height and armspan

Measure the height and armspan of some people.
Record the measurements in **metres**.

Look at the heights and armspans you recorded.
Is one always greater than the other?

F Ordering decimals

F1 Which of these numbers are between 2.3 and 2.5?

2.35	2.55	2.4
	2.25	2.04

F2 Which of these numbers are between 5 and 5.2?

0.51	5.17	5.03
	5.1	5.21

F3 Write each list in order of size, smallest first.

(a) 5.32, 5.84, 6, 5.09, 5.76

(b) 3.2, 3.07, 2.8, 3.19, 3.5

(c) 0.6, 0.15, 1.07, 1.1, 0.45

F4 Spell a word by arranging the numbers in order, smallest first.

A	D	O	L	I	S	H	Y
0.36	0.2	0.08	0.1	0.16	0.41	0.03	0.4

F5 Spell another word by arranging these numbers in order.

J	A	B	O	N	E	L	E	Y
1.57	1.96	2.05	1.6	1.3	1.14	2.26	2.4	1.8

F6 Spell a word by arranging these numbers in order.

S	O	R	U	D	A	N	I
0.61	0.6	1.5	1.07	0.08	0.9	0.54	0.2

F7 This table gives the results of a long jump contest.

Name	1st jump	2nd jump	3rd jump
Singh	3.92 m	4.36 m	4.5 m
Barker	4.2 m	4.13 m	3.87 m
Church	4.18 m	4.4 m	4.12 m

(a) How long was Barker's longest jump?

(b) Whose 1st jump was longest?

(c) Whose 2nd jump was longest?

(d) What was the length of the longest jump of all?

G Place value

thousands hundreds tens units tenths hundredths

2 7 1 3 . 5 8

Do not use a calculator in this section.

G1 The figure 5 in the number 2713.58 above stands for 5 tenths, or 0.5
What do these figures stand for?

(a) The 7   (b) The 2   (c) The 3   (d) The 1   (e) The 8

G2 Do these in your head.

(a) Add a ten to 2713.58   (b) Add a thousand to 2713.58

(c) Add a tenth to 2713.58   (d) Add a unit to 2713.58

(e) Add a hundredth to 2713.58   (f) Add a hundred to 2713.58

G3 Do these in your head.

(a) Add 100 to 1426.35   (b) Add 1 to 1426.35

(c) Add 0.1 to 1426.35   (d) Add 1000 to 1426.35

(e) Add 10 to 1426.35   (f) Add 0.01 to 1426.35

G4 What do these figures stand for?

(a) The 7 in 16.72   (b) The 3 in 4.03   (c) The 6 in 2364.81

(d) The 8 in 735.82   (e) The 4 in 320.04   (f) The 5 in 13.58

G5 Jason started with the number **463.86**.
He subtracted something and ended up with **403.86**.
What number did he subtract?

G6 Pam started with **248.71**.
She subtracted a number and ended up with **248.01**.
What number did she subtract?

G7 Grant started with **54.73**.
He subtracted a number and ended up with **54.7**.
What did he subtract?

What progress have you made?

Statement

Evidence

I can read scales to two decimal places.

1 What number does each arrow point to?

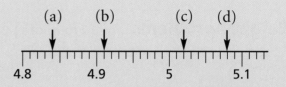

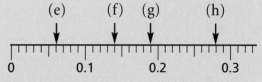

I can use decimals of a metre.

2 (a) Write 1 metre 45 centimetres in metres.

(b) Write 2 metres 3 centimetres in metres.

(c) Write 3.2 metres in metres and centimetres.

I can order numbers with up to two decimal places.

3 Write each list of numbers in order of size, smallest first.

(a) 7.3, 6.68, 6.9, 7.04, 6.7

(b) 3.24, 0.07, 0.1, 4, 1.56

I know what the figures in decimal numbers stand for.

4 What do these figures stand for?

(a) The 8 in 12.83

(b) The 4 in 23.04

(c) The 7 in 100.67

34 Practical problems

This work will help you measure and estimate quantities.

Weighty problems for a group of pupils

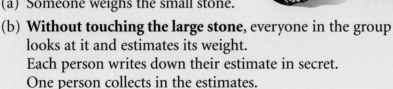

1   There are two stones.

   (a) Someone weighs the small stone.

   (b) **Without touching the large stone**, everyone in the group
       looks at it and estimates its weight.
       Each person writes down their estimate in secret.
       One person collects in the estimates.

   (c) Now someone weighs the large stone.
       Everyone compares their estimates with the weight of the stone.
       They record everybody's estimates and the real weight.

2   Now everyone looks at the set of objects.

   (a) **Without touching them**, everyone in the group decides
       what order of weight they should go in.
       Each person writes down their order in secret.

   (b) Now people can touch the objects.
       Without weighing them on the scales, each person
       writes the objects in order of weight again, in secret.
       One person collects in both sets of estimates.

   (c) Now someone weighs the objects.
       Each person compares their two orders of weight with the real order.

Beans for pupils working individually

Estimate the number of beans in the jar.

Write down how you worked out your estimate
and any measurements that you made.

Cornflakes for pupils working individually

1 (a) Get a cereal bowl.
Put into it enough cornflakes for a reasonable breakfast.
Weigh this amount.

  (b) Weigh out the suggested portion size given on the box.
How does this portion compare with your portion?

2 (a) Work out how many portions you can pour from
the box if they are the recommended size.

  (b) How many portions can you pour from the box if
they are your size?

3 (a) Work out the cost of the recommended portion.

  (b) Work out the cost of your own portion.

Getting better for pupils working individually

You have three bottles. Suppose each one is filled with medicine.

1 Look at these instructions.

> **Take one 5 ml spoonful**
> **3 times a day.**

How long will each of the three bottles last?

2 How long will each bottle last with this prescription?

> **Take two 5 ml spoonfuls**
> **twice a day.**

3 You are told to take two 5 ml spoonfuls 4 times a day for 20 days.
Would any of your three bottles be big enough?

Children's TV for pupils working individually

You have a friend abroad.
You want to show them what children's TV is like in Britain.

You decide to record a video.
You want to record some typical programmes on a
three-hour tape.

Choose some children's programmes to record.
Choose a mixture of different types and different lengths.
Don't just choose your favourite programmes!

Try to use as much of the three-hour tape as possible.

Write down

- the names of the programmes

- how long each one lasts

- the total time of your recording

Windfall for pupils working individually

A rich relative has given you £150 to spend!

You definitely want a watch,
a Walkman and a bag.

You can buy anything else you want.

But you must make the total you spend
as close to £150 as possible.

Decide on your shopping list.

Record the catalogue numbers, the prices and the total cost.

35 Amazing but true!

This will remind you of work you
have done with coordinates.

On 22nd July 1998 a maze designer opened
the world's biggest maze in Sussex, England.

He designed the maze on a computer and
used a grid to tell his helpers how to make the maze.

The maze below has also been designed using a grid.

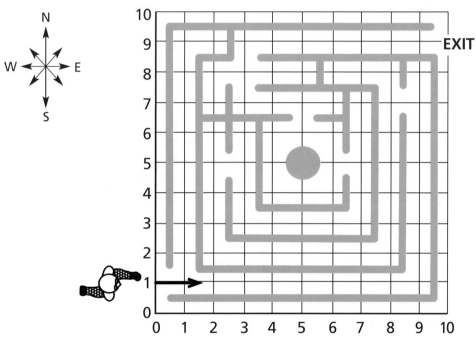

Here is the start of the instructions for getting through the maze.

Start at (0, 1)	Go east
At (9, 1)	Go north
At (9, 7)	Go west

Copy and complete the instructions to go through the maze.

Design a maze of your own on a 10 by 10 grid.
Ask a friend to work out the instructions to get through.
Get them to read out their instructions and you check them.

36 Is it an add?

This work will help you decide which calculations to do when you have problems to solve.

A Add, subtract, multiply or divide?

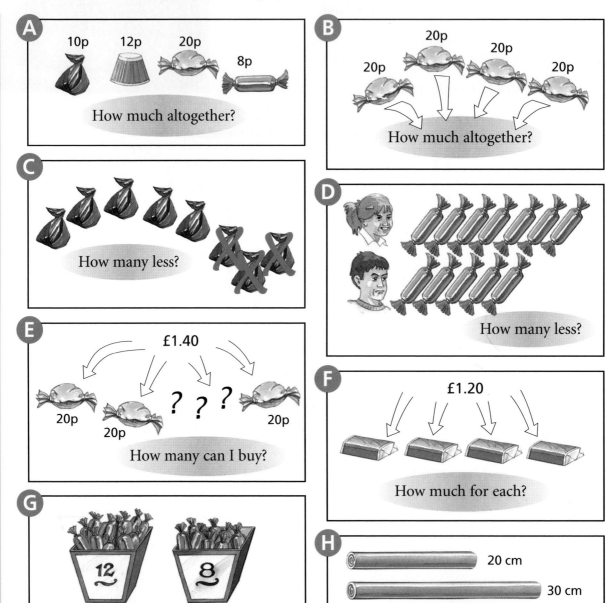

A

10p   12p   20p   8p

How much altogether?

B

20p   20p   20p   20p

How much altogether?

C

How many less?

D

How many less?

E

£1.40

20p   20p   ? ? ?   20p

How many can I buy?

F

£1.20

How much for each?

G

12   8

How many altogether?

H

20 cm
30 cm

What's the difference in length?

Calculations

$20 - 4$ $20 + 4$ $4 \div 20$ 20×4 $4 - 20$ $20 \div 4$

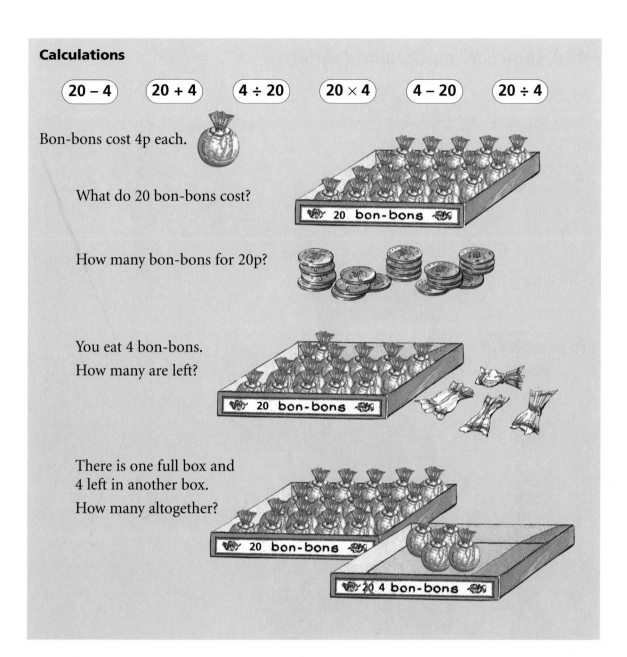

Bon-bons cost 4p each.

What do 20 bon-bons cost?

How many bon-bons for 20p?

You eat 4 bon-bons.
How many are left?

There is one full box and
4 left in another box.
How many altogether?

Calculations

$36 - 4$ 4×36 $4 \div 36$ 36×4 $36 \div 4$ $4 - 36$

Satya buys some bon-bons.
They cost 36p altogether.
How many does she buy?

Usha buys 36 bon-bons.
What do they cost altogether?

213

Add, subtract, multiply or divide?

Fit a calculation to each question opposite.

nutto
20p

Calculations

8 + 20	80 × 8	80 ÷ 20	80 − 20
20 + 80	80 − 8	8 × 20	20 ÷ 8
20 × 8	20 × 80	80 ÷ 8	20 − 8

toffee
8p

20 × 12	12 × 8	20 ÷ 12	12 − 8
12 + 8	12 ÷ 20	12 ÷ 8	20 − 12
20 + 12	8 ÷ 12	8 × 12	8 + 12

cream
12p

12 ÷ 120	12 − 8	12 × 8	12 × 120
12 ÷ 8	120 × 12	12 + 8	120 ÷ 8
120 − 12	8 × 12	120 ÷ 12	120 × 8

fudge
30p

Mixed box
(30 of each)

30 × 120	20 − 8	30 ÷ 12	30 − 12
20 × 8	30 × 12	30 + 12	120 − 30
12 ÷ 30	20 + 8	120 ÷ 30	20 ÷ 8
120 + 30	12 − 30	30 ÷ 120	12 × 30

Questions

A1 What do 8 nuttos cost?

A2 How many boxes of nuttos can you fill if you have 80 nuttos?

A3 How many nuttos could you buy for 80p?

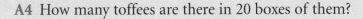

A4 How many toffees are there in 20 boxes of them?

A5 How much does a box of toffees cost?

A6 How many sweets are there altogether in a box of nuttos and a box of toffees?

A7 How much do you have to pay for 8 creams?

A8 How many creams are there in a box?

A9 How much more do you pay for one cream than one toffee?

A10 You eat 8 fudges from a box of fudges.
     How many are left?

A11 What do 12 fudges cost?

A12 You eat 12 creams from a mixed box.
     How many creams are left in the mixed box?

A13 The whirls in a mixed box cost £1.20.
     How much does one whirl cost?

215

B Video cassettes

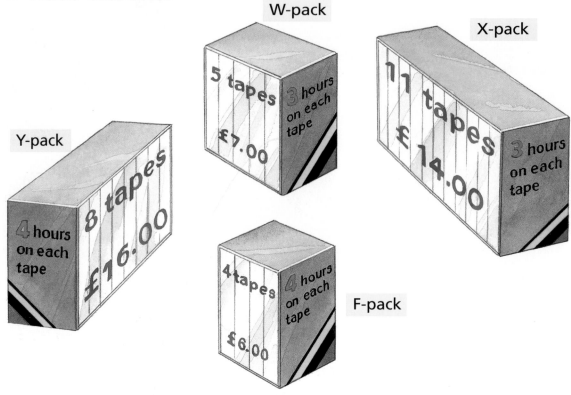

Write the calculation for each question.

B1 How many hours do you get in a W-pack?

B2 What is the cost of one tape from an F-pack?

B3 What would an F-pack and a Y-pack cost together?

B4 What is the difference in price between a Y-pack and an X-pack?

B5 How much would you have to pay for four X-packs?

B6 How many more tapes are there in an X-pack than a Y-pack?

B7 If you buy a W-pack and a Y-pack, how many tapes do you get?

B8 How many tapes are in five Y-packs?

B9 You record a one-and-a-half hour programme on a tape from an F-pack. How much time is left on the tape?

B10 How many tapes from a W-pack would you need to record 15 hours of TV?

C Telling tales

C1 Here is a 'tale' with a question.

> *Paul wants to buy 20 cans of Fizzo.*
> *The cans come in packs of four.*
> *How many packs does he need to buy?*

Which of these calculations goes with the tale?

$20 + 4$ 20×4 $20 - 4$ $20 \div 4$ $4 \div 20$

C2 Write down the calculation that goes with each of these tales.

(a) *Ellie has 35 soft toys on her bed.*
She gives 23 away to a charity
for refugee children.
How many soft toys has she left?

(b) *Nasser has 96 tapes.*
He wants to store them in racks.
Each rack holds 12 tapes.
How many racks does he need?

(c) *Mark has 15 calves in a herd of cows.*
One night 8 more calves are born.
How many calves are there now?

(d) *Ms King checks brushes for her art lesson.*
There are 18 pupils in the class.
She needs five brushes for each pupil.
How many brushes does she need?

C3 Write a tale with a question for each of these calculations.

(a) 6×4 (b) $24 \div 3$ (c) $30 - 12$ (d) $12 + 8$

D Check it out

You will need a calculator in this section.

Some pupils are discussing ways of checking answers.

> *When I add up a list of numbers*
> *I always check my answer by*
> *adding again in reverse order.*

> *I always check*
> *subtractions by adding.*
> *So 367 – 286 = 81*
> *Check: 286 + 81 = 367*

> *Multiplication is the same*
> *either way round.*
> *You can use this to check.*
> *24 × 56 = 1344*
> *Check: 56 × 24 = 1344*

> *Multiplying is the opposite*
> *of dividing so use this to check.*
> *192 ÷ 12 = 16*
> *Check: 12 × 16 = 192*

Are there any other ways you could check your answers?

D1 Do these on a calculator and check each answer.
Write down the calculation you did to check your answer.

  (a) 259 + 472   (b) 235 + 356 + 192   (c) 2125 + 764 + 515

  (d) 354 − 187   (e) 2008 − 1876   (f) 37 × 64

  (g) 237 × 48   (h) 374 ÷ 17   (i) 1524 ÷ 254

In the rest of the questions in this section

  • write down the calculation you are going to do

  • work out the answer with a calculator

  • check your answer

D2

  Zebra 267 kg   Kangaroo 86 kg   Hippo 3825 kg   Tiger 228 kg

  (a) How much do these four animals weigh altogether?

  (b) How much heavier is a zebra than a tiger?

  (c) How much would eight zebras weigh altogether?

D3 Jill has a plank of wood 237 cm long.
She cuts off a piece 128 cm long.
How long is the piece of the plank remaining?

D4 Some workmen are laying pipes. Each pipe is 18 metres long.
They need to have 414 metres of pipe altogether. How many pipes do they need?

D5 Mr Bliss has four cows.
He keeps a record of how many litres of milk each cow gives.
This is his record for four weeks in July.

Name	1st week	2nd week	3rd week	4th week
Abigail	137	141	131	137
Buttercup	126	134	130	132
Cowslip	136	133	139	137
Daisy	138	143	143	139

  (a) How many litres of milk did Abigail give altogether in these four weeks?

  (b) Which cow gave the most milk altogether in the four weeks?

  (c) In which of the four weeks did Mr Bliss get the most milk?

D6 (a) An office block has 27 floors. Each floor has 36 windows.
How many windows does the office block have altogether?

(b) Another office block has 22 windows on each floor.
There are 396 windows altogether.
How many floors does this office block have?

*D7 (a) Sharon is paid £5.62 per hour in her job.
How much does she get paid for working 38 hours?

(b) One week Sharon earns £241.66.
How many hours did she work that week?

Challenge

A van can carry a maximum weight of 1000 kg.
At the depot there are boxes with these weights.

 A:423 kg   B:371 kg   C:535 kg   D:134 kg   E:208 kg   F:89 kg

Which boxes should be loaded to give the greatest weight
without going over the maximum?

What progress have you made?

Statement

I can choose the right calculation for a problem.

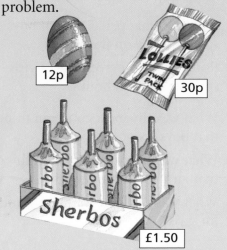

Evidence

1 Write the calculation that goes with each of these questions from this picture.

(a) How much would 6 eggs cost?

(b) What is the cost of one Sherbo in a tray?

(c) How much more does the lollies twin pack cost than an egg?

(d) Angie buys a box of Sherbos and a lollies twin pack.
How much do they cost altogether?

2 Write the calculation for this tale.

Mary has 6 cats.
They each eat 4 tins of tuna a week.
How many tins do they eat altogether in a week?

3 Do these on a calculator.
Write down how you checked your answer.

(a) 175 + 342 + 218   (b) 29 × 35

37 Graphs and charts

This is about displaying information.
The work will help you read and draw
graphs and charts.

A Children's income

This picture shows the regions of Great Britain
and the results of a survey of children's income.

What information is given for each region?

How does your region compare with other regions?

A1 (a) What is the largest amount of
income shown?

(b) Where did children get most income?

(c) Where did children get least income?

(d) What is the difference between the greatest
and smallest amounts?

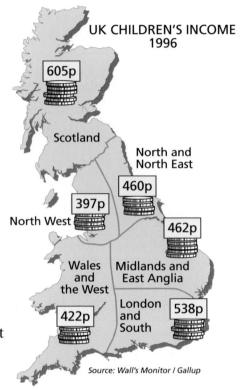

UK CHILDREN'S INCOME
1996

605p

Scotland

North and
North East

460p

397p

North West

462p

Wales
and
the West

Midlands and
East Anglia

London
and
South

422p

538p

Source: Wall's Monitor / Gallup

The bar chart shows the results of a survey of boys' and girls' spending.
For example, it shows that about 65% of boys spent money on sweets.

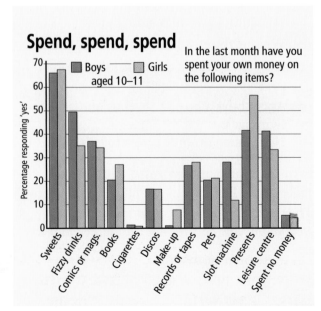

Spend, spend, spend

In the last month have you
spent your own money on
the following items?

Boys — Girls
aged 10–11

Percentage responding 'yes'

Sweets, Fizzy drinks, Comics or mags., Books, Cigarettes, Discos, Make-up, Records or tapes, Pets, Slot machine, Presents, Leisure centre, Spent no money

A2 (a) Roughly what percentage of boys
spent money on fizzy drinks?

(b) Roughly what percentage of girls
spent money on books?

A3 (a) What was the most common thing
that boys spent money on?

(b) What was the most common thing
that girls spent money on?

(c) What was the least common thing
for girls?

A4 How many pupils were surveyed?

A5 What have you spent your own money
on during the last month?

B Shut up!

This graph is about the number of complaints made about noise.

Complaints about noise

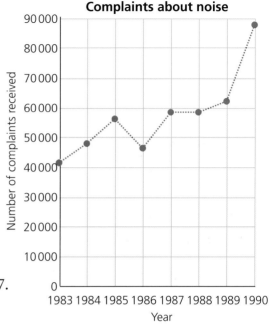

B1 (a) In what year was the highest number of complaints made?

   (b) (i) In which two years were there the same number of complaints?

   (ii) About how many complaints were made in each of these years?

   (c) Between which two years did the number of complaints actually drop?

   (d) Between which two years did the number of complaints rise the most?

B2 Complaints went up between 1986 and 1987. By how many roughly?

B3 Copy and complete this story

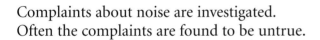

Between 1983 and 1985 complaints rose steadily. Then ...

Complaints about noise are investigated. Often the complaints are found to be untrue.

This graph shows the number of complaints found to be true.

Complaints found to be true

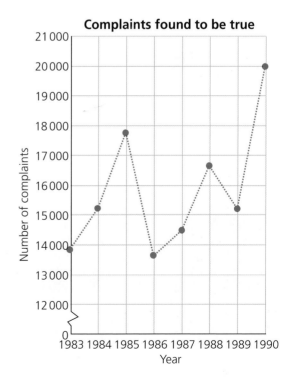

B4 Look closely at the numbering on the vertical scale.

Why is there a jagged line at the bottom of the scale, between 0 and 12 000?

B5 Between which two years was there the biggest drop in complaints found to be true?

B6 In what year was there the lowest number of complaints found to be true?

C Off the record

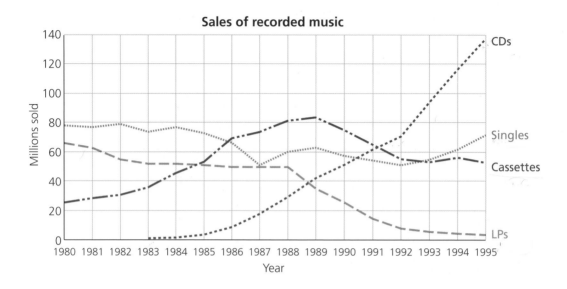

Sales of recorded music

Millions sold (y-axis: 0, 20, 40, 60, 80, 100, 120, 140)

Year (x-axis: 1980, 1981, 1982, 1983, 1984, 1985, 1986, 1987, 1988, 1989, 1990, 1991, 1992, 1993, 1994, 1995)

CDs
Singles
Cassettes
LPs

C1 Between 1980 and 1995, the sales of LPs dropped,
stayed steady then went down again.

(a) What happened to the sales of CDs?

(b) What happened to the sales of cassettes?

(c) When did CD sales overtake LP sales?

(d) When did cassette sales first reach 70 million?

(e) Roughly how many singles were sold in 1982?

C2 Make up two questions of your own about this graph.
Give them to someone else to answer.

Do their answers agree with yours?

D Equal shares

A survey is carried out every few years on who does what at home.
Here are the results from the 1991 survey.

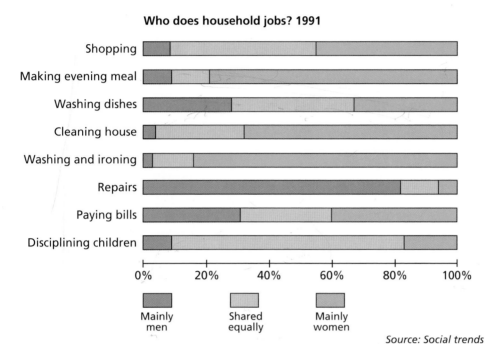

Who does household jobs? 1991

Source: Social trends

D1 Which job had the highest percentage of

(a) 'mainly men'

(b) 'mainly women'

D2 What job was done least by men?
Explain how you can tell this from the graph.

D3 What jobs were done by 'mainly women' in more
than half of all homes?

D4 Which job had the highest percentage of 'shared equally'?

D5 Which jobs were roughly evenly split between men and women?
Explain how you can tell this from the graph.

E Drawing graphs and charts

Frequency bar charts

Pupils' test scores

37	41	28	60	56
39	17	39	73	64
58	25	44	66	34
32	78	35	46	76
18	39	56	38	75
53	49	55	38	47
53	86	34	64	26
36	22	18	73	9

Drawing frequency bar charts

1   Draw up a tally chart.
2   Fill in tally marks for the data.
3   Fill in the frequency column.
4   Draw and label axes.
5   Draw bars.
6   Write title on chart.

Represent each of these sets of data in a frequency bar chart.
For each one, a suitable tally chart is started.

E1 Ages of people living in a village

41	25	75	64	14	9	23	64
69	33	53	51	27	38	70	22
66	40	38	41	77	80	38	44
13	53	22	59	52	71	60	25

Age group	Tally	Frequency
0–9		
10–19		
20–29		
30–		

E2 Number of cars using a car park each day

54	67	52	74	109	75	86	65
83	100	111	104	67	84	92	74
82	84	89	117	52	95	59	97
92	66	88	94	107	82	57	56
85	98	117	93	68	94	84	77

Number of cars	Tally	Frequency
50–59		
60–69		
70–79		
80–		

E3 Reaction times of pupils using a reaction ruler

20	18	18	13	15	16	17	17
18	22	17	15	11	12	12	13
17	18	21	19	15	16	10	11
16	15	20	16	26	14		

Reaction time (hundredths of a second)	Tally	Frequency
10–12		
13–15		
16–18		
19–		

Line graphs

Temperature of oven in °C at 1 minute intervals
from switching on

Time in minutes	0	1	2	3	4	5	6	7	8
Temperature in °C	20	68	129	157	173	184	192	196	198

Drawing line graphs

1 Draw and label axes.

2 Plot points.

3 Join up the points.

4 Write title of graph.

Represent these sets of data as line graphs.

E4 This table shows the number of new cases of flu in a fortnight.
Draw your across axis from 0 to 14, and your vertical axis from 0 to 26.

Day	1	2	3	4	5	6	7	8	9	10	11	12	13	14
Cases	3	7	8	11	16	24	22	26	19	15	15	7	3	1

E5 These are the noon temperatures at Rownhams in the first two weeks of December.
Draw your across axis from 0 to 14, and your vertical axis from 0 to 16.

Day in December	1	2	3	4	5	6	7	8	9	10	11	12	13	14
Temperature in °C	15	16	16	12	11	6	3	4	6	8	7	10	9	9

What progress have you made?

Statement

I can read a bar chart.

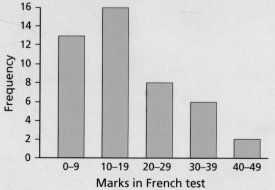

Evidence

1 (a) How many children in this class got less
than 10 marks in their French test?

(b) How many got between 20 and 29 marks?

Statement	Evidence

Statement

I can read a line graph.

Evidence

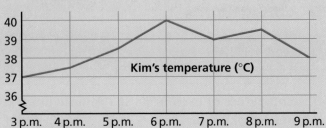

2 (a) What was Kim's temperature at 4:30 p.m?

   (b) Describe what happened to Kim's temperature between 3 p.m. and 9 p.m.

I can draw a line graph.

3 This table shows the number of babies born in a hospital in the first 10 days of June.

Day	1	2	3	4	5	6	7	8	9	10
Babies	6	8	7	12	3	4	9	11	12	9

Draw a line graph showing this data.

Make your across axis go from 0 to 10 and your vertical axis go from 0 to 12.

I can use tallying to make a grouped frequency table.

4 Here are the ages of the people in a village.

30   23   43   75   63   71   18   25
11   9   66   28   7   22   68   29
55   29   12   40   37   69   70   32
71   8   14

Copy and complete this tally chart.

Age group	Tally	Frequency
0–9		
10–19		
20–29		
30–		

I can draw a bar chart.

5 Draw a bar chart for the data in question 4.

Oral questions: money 2

This work will help you

◆ choose the information you need to solve a problem

◆ answer spoken questions

Here is a page from a stationery catalogue.

STATIONERY

Sticky tape **£1.19**

Ruler **£0.79**

Pencils 6 pack **£0.67**

Scissors **£3.15**

Stapler **£7.80**

Correcting fluid **£1.15**

Hole punch **£8.50**

Ink cartridges **£1.07**

Pencil Case **£1.10**

Note pad **£0.57**

Eraser **£0.15**

Geometry Set **£5.33**

Stick-it notes **£2.14**

Colouring pencils **£3.20**

Page 162

39 Working with fractions

7S/10, 7S/54

This work will help you work out fractions of numbers.

A Chocolate

B Simple fractions of numbers

Halving a number is the same as dividing it by 2

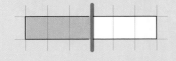 

$\frac{1}{2}$ of 6 = 3

6 ÷ 2 = 3

$\frac{1}{2}$ of 8 = 4

8 ÷ 2 = 4

Finding $\frac{1}{4}$ of a number is the same as dividing it by 4

In this chocolate bar, 12 pieces are split into 4 equal groups.

This bar is also split into 4 equal groups.

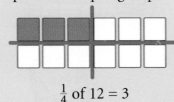   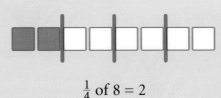

$\frac{1}{4}$ of 12 = 3

12 ÷ 4 = 3

$\frac{1}{4}$ of 8 = 2

8 ÷ 4 = 2

B1 Work these out.

(a) $\frac{1}{2}$ of 4   (b) $\frac{1}{2}$ of 14   (c) $\frac{1}{2}$ of 22   (d) $\frac{1}{2}$ of 10   (e) $\frac{1}{2}$ of 36

B2 Work these out.

(a) $\frac{1}{4}$ of 8   (b) $\frac{1}{4}$ of 32   (c) $\frac{1}{4}$ of 24   (d) $\frac{1}{4}$ of 40   (e) $\frac{1}{4}$ of 52

B3 This chocolate bar shows $\frac{1}{3}$ of 6.

$\frac{1}{3}$ of 6 pieces is 2 pieces.

$\frac{1}{3}$ of 6 = 2

Match each statement below with its chocolate bar.

P $\frac{1}{3}$ of 12 = 4

Q $\frac{1}{6}$ of 18 = 3

R $\frac{1}{2}$ of 12 = 6

S $\frac{1}{4}$ of 12 = 3

T $\frac{1}{3}$ of 18 = 6

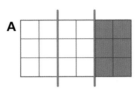

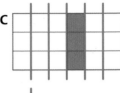

B4 Draw chocolate bars to show each of these.

(a) $\frac{1}{4}$ of 16 = 4　　(b) $\frac{1}{3}$ of 24 = 8　　(c) $\frac{1}{5}$ of 15 = 3　　(d) $\frac{1}{6}$ of 24 = 4

B5 Work these out.

(a) $\frac{1}{2}$ of 16　　(b) $\frac{1}{3}$ of 21　　(c) $\frac{1}{4}$ of 36　　(d) $\frac{1}{5}$ of 10　　(e) $\frac{1}{8}$ of 72

B6 Work these out.

Use a calculator if you need to.

(a) $\frac{1}{2}$ of 1564　　　　(b) $\frac{1}{4}$ of 1972　　　　(c) $\frac{1}{3}$ of 23 607

(d) $\frac{1}{7}$ of 366 387　　　(e) $\frac{1}{8}$ of 2072　　　　(f) $\frac{1}{10}$ of 258 970

(g) $\frac{1}{100}$ of 12 967 000　(h) $\frac{1}{12}$ of 5472　　　　(i) $\frac{1}{6}$ of 3798

B7 About $\frac{1}{100}$ of all females are colour blind.

349 600 females were born in the UK in 1991.
Roughly how many of these babies were colour blind?

B8 The largest biscuit ever made contained 4 million chocolate chips.
$\frac{1}{8}$ of them were white.

How many of the chocolate chips were white?

B9 The longest paper chain ever made had 400 000 links.
One person made $\frac{1}{50}$ of these.

How many links did that person make?

B10 There were 150 000 people at the largest feast ever held.
$\frac{1}{12}$ of these people were vegetarians.

How many vegetarians were at the feast?

C Other fractions of numbers

$\frac{3}{4}$ is 3 times $\frac{1}{4}$

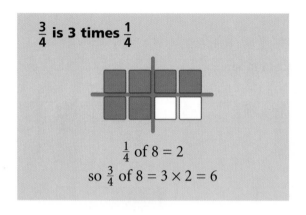

$\frac{1}{4}$ of 8 = 2

so $\frac{3}{4}$ of 8 = 3 × 2 = 6

$\frac{2}{3}$ is 2 times $\frac{1}{3}$

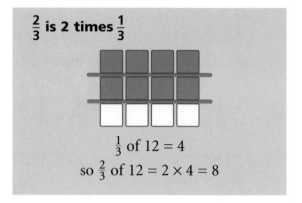

$\frac{1}{3}$ of 12 = 4

so $\frac{2}{3}$ of 12 = 2 × 4 = 8

Try to do each of these questions without using a calculator.

C1 Work these out.

(a) $\frac{3}{4}$ of 24   (b) $\frac{3}{4}$ of 32   (c) $\frac{3}{4}$ of 40   (d) $\frac{3}{4}$ of 4   (e) $\frac{3}{4}$ of 44

C2 Work these out.

(a) $\frac{2}{3}$ of 24   (b) $\frac{2}{3}$ of 30   (c) $\frac{2}{3}$ of 18   (d) $\frac{2}{3}$ of 21   (e) $\frac{2}{3}$ of 33

C3 Match each statement below with one of the diagrams.

P $\frac{3}{4}$ of 24 = 18

Q $\frac{3}{5}$ of 20 = 12

R $\frac{2}{3}$ of 18 = 12

S $\frac{3}{4}$ of 20 = 15

T $\frac{5}{6}$ of 24 = 20

U $\frac{5}{6}$ of 18 = 15

A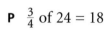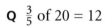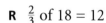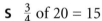

B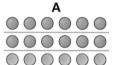

C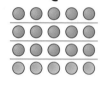

D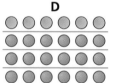

E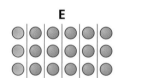

F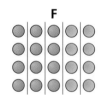

C4 Work these out.

(a) $\frac{3}{4}$ of 36   (b) $\frac{2}{5}$ of 30   (c) $\frac{3}{8}$ of 40   (d) $\frac{5}{6}$ of 42   (e) $\frac{2}{3}$ of 60

C5 Leontina Albina, who lived in Chile, had 40 surviving children. $\frac{2}{5}$ of them were girls. How many were girls?

C6 Jack is 180 cm tall and 36 years old.

(a) Zoe is $\frac{8}{9}$ of Jack's height. How tall is Zoe?

(b) Zoe's age is $\frac{2}{3}$ of Jack's age. How old is Zoe?

Use a calculator for these questions if you need to.

C7 Work these out.

(a) $\frac{2}{3}$ of 792   (b) $\frac{4}{5}$ of 4610   (c) $\frac{7}{10}$ of 4000   (d) $\frac{3}{4}$ of 492 000

C8 The main lift shaft at the Empire State Building is 320 m high.
In January 2000 a lift fell $\frac{2}{5}$ of the way down the shaft. No one was hurt!
How far did the lift fall?

C9 About 375 000 people live in Bristol.
Roughly $\frac{4}{5}$ of this number of people live in Coventry.
About how many people live in Coventry?

C10 The area of France is 544 000 km².

(a) The area of Ireland is $\frac{1}{8}$ the area of France.
What is the area of Ireland?

(b) The area of Finland is $\frac{5}{8}$ the area of France.
What is the area of Finland?

C11 A small beech tree has approximately 2000 leaves.
$\frac{3}{10}$ of the leaves fell off one autumn. About how many leaves fell?

D Improper fractions and mixed numbers

There are seven $\frac{1}{4}$ s here.   Together they make $1\frac{3}{4}$.

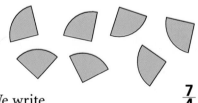   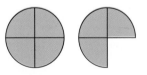

We write $\frac{7}{4}$ = $1\frac{3}{4}$

$\frac{7}{4}$ is called an **improper fraction**. $1\frac{3}{4}$ is called a **mixed number**.

D1 (a) (i) How many $\frac{1}{4}$ s are there here?

(ii) Write it as a mixed number.

(b) Copy and complete.

$$\frac{5}{4} = \text{.......}$$

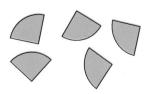

D2 (a) How many $\frac{1}{4}$ s are there here?

(b) Copy and complete. $2\frac{1}{4} = \frac{}{4}$

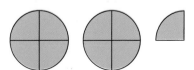

D3 Copy and complete each of these.

(a) $3\frac{1}{4} = \frac{}{4}$ (b) $3\frac{3}{4} = \frac{}{4}$ (c) $\frac{17}{4} = 4\frac{}{4}$ (d) $\frac{21}{4} = \ldots$

D4 Olive oil comes in $\frac{1}{3}$ litre cans.

(a) There are five cans here.
Write the amount of oil as
an improper fraction.

(b) Write the amount of oil here as a mixed number.

D5 Copy and complete each of these.

(a) $\frac{4}{3} = 1\frac{}{3}$ (b) $2\frac{2}{3} = \frac{}{3}$ (c) $2\frac{1}{3} = \frac{}{3}$ (d) $\frac{10}{3} = \ldots$

D6 Write each of these as a mixed number.

(a) $\frac{3}{2}$ (b) $\frac{5}{2}$ (c) $\frac{8}{5}$ (d) $\frac{12}{5}$ (e) $\frac{10}{7}$

D7 Write each of these as an improper fraction.

(a) $3\frac{1}{2}$ (b) $6\frac{1}{2}$ (c) $8\frac{1}{3}$ (d) $6\frac{2}{3}$ (e) $2\frac{1}{7}$

What progress have you made?

Statement	Evidence
I can work out simple fractions of numbers.	**1** Work these out. (a) $\frac{1}{2}$ of 18 (b) $\frac{1}{4}$ of 20 (c) $\frac{1}{5}$ of 30 **2** Work these out. (a) $\frac{1}{8}$ of 72 (b) $\frac{1}{7}$ of 35 (c) $\frac{1}{6}$ of 60 **3** Use a calculator to work these out. (a) $\frac{1}{4}$ of 220 (b) $\frac{1}{5}$ of 1000 (c) $\frac{1}{6}$ of 756
I can work out more difficult fractions of numbers.	**4** Work these out. (a) $\frac{2}{3}$ of 21 (b) $\frac{3}{4}$ of 80 (c) $\frac{3}{5}$ of 35 **5** Use a calculator to work these out. (a) $\frac{3}{7}$ of 300 272 (b) $\frac{4}{11}$ of 7392 (c) $\frac{3}{5}$ of 855 (d) $\frac{7}{12}$ of 1440
I understand mixed numbers and improper fractions.	**6** Copy and complete each of these. (a) $\frac{11}{3} = \ldots$ (b) $\frac{9}{2} = \ldots$ (c) $\frac{9}{5} = \ldots$ (d) $1\frac{1}{5} = \frac{}{5}$ (e) $4\frac{1}{3} = \frac{}{3}$ (f) $1\frac{5}{6} = \frac{}{6}$

⃝40 3-D shapes

This work will help you

◆ recognise the nets of an open cube

◆ solve problems with 3-D shapes using 2-D drawings

A Pentominoes

A pentomino is made
with five squares.

Squares are joined together
edge to edge like this.

These are not allowed.

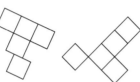

- Find the pentominoes made by adding
  one more square to this.

- Find all the other pentominoes.

- How can you be sure you have found them all?

- How can you be sure you have not found the
  same pentomino twice?

The 8 by 8 game   for two or three players

You need sheets 56 and 57.

- Cut out the set of pentominoes on sheet 56.

- Take turns to place a pentomino on the board (sheet 57).
  You must not overlap any pentomino already on the board.

- The winner is the last player to place a pentomino on the board.

B Nets

This pentomino …   can be folded …   to make an open cube.

B1 Which of these pentominoes can be folded to make an open cube?

(a) 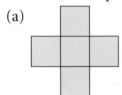   (b) 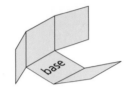   (c)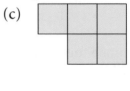

(d) 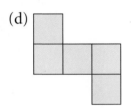   (e)    (f)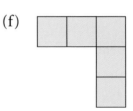

B2 This pentomino is folded to make an open cube with the numbers on the outside.

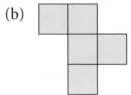

Say whether these are possible views of the open cube it makes.

(a) 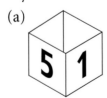   (b) 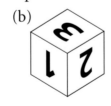   (c) 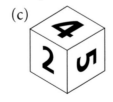   (d)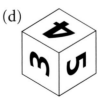

Design a poster

Any pentomino which can be folded to make a solid shape is a **net** of that shape.
There are 8 different designs for the net of an open cube.
You have seen some already. Find them all.

Design a poster to show all the possible nets for an open cube.

C Seeing in 3-D

Four cubes

An activity for small groups

This 3-D shape is made from four cubes.

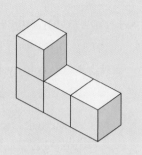

- How many different shapes can you make with four cubes? Cubes must be joined by a face.
- Compare your shapes with others in the group.
- Make a collection of all the **different** shapes.

C1 These shapes are all made from five cubes.
Match them into four pairs which are the same shape.

 A
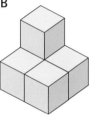 B
 C
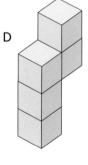 D

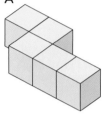

 E
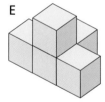 F
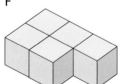 G
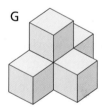 H
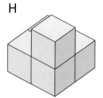

C2 Three of these are drawings of the same shape made from five cubes.
Which is the odd one out?

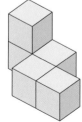 P
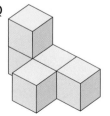 Q
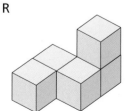 R
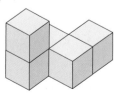 S

235

C3 A cuboid is a solid rectangular box.
    Make a cuboid that is 4 cubes long by 3 cubes wide and 2 cubes high.
    How many cubes do you need to make this?

C4 How many cubes would you need to make cuboids with these measurements?

    (a) 3 cubes long by 3 cubes wide and 4 cubes high

    (b) 4 cubes long by 5 cubes wide and 3 cubes high

    (c) 10 cubes long by 8 cubes wide and 5 cubes high

C5 Ms White asks her class to make a cuboid which is
    3 cubes wide by 3 cubes long and 2 cubes high.

    These are some unfinished cuboids.
    There are no hidden gaps.
    How many cubes does each pupil need to finish their cuboid?

David

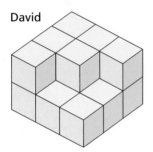

Susan

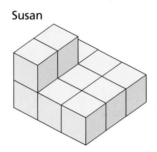

Spencer

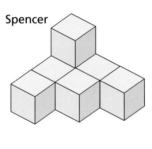

C6 Mr Platt asks his class to make a large cube
    with each side 3 cubes long.

    How many cubes does each pupil need to finish their cube?

Meena

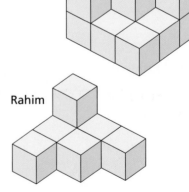

Peter

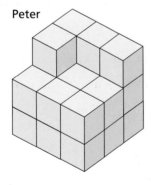

Ros

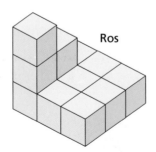

Rahim

C7 Mr Anthony's class decide to make a copy of the famous Hollywood sign in cubes. Each letter is to be 5 cubes high and 2 cubes thick.

How many more cubes are needed to finish each of these?

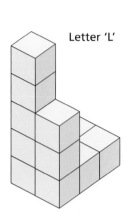

Letter 'L'

Letter 'H'

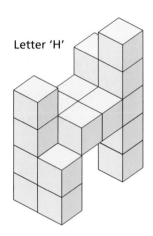

Letter 'O'

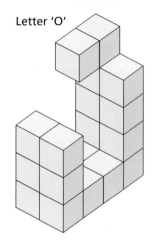

What progress have you made?

Statement

I can recognise the net of an open cube.

Evidence

1 Which of these are nets for an open cube?

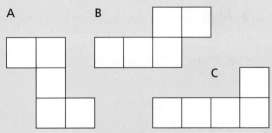

A   B   C

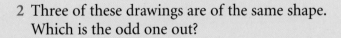

I can recognise 3-D shapes from 2-D drawings.

2 Three of these drawings are of the same shape. Which is the odd one out?

E   F   G   H

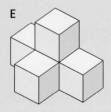 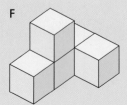 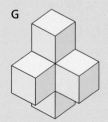 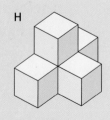

 Ratio

This work will help you solve simple ratio problems.

A Recipes

Pumpkin soup *serves 2 people*
300 g pumpkin
50 g butter
1 bay leaf
100 ml milk
60 ml single cream
salt and pepper

Pizza topping *makes 1 pizza*
450 g ripe tomatoes
200 g mushrooms
12 olives
4 tablespoons olive oil
2 medium onions
1 clove of garlic
1 tablespoon of tomato puree
40 g grated parmesan cheese

Pancakes *makes 5 pancakes*
125 g plain flour
1 egg
300 ml milk
a pinch of salt
25 g lard

Sheek kebabs *makes 4 kebabs*
700 g minced beef
4 cm piece of fresh ginger
2 fresh chillies
2 tablespoons fresh coriander
6 cloves of garlic
1 teaspoon dried mint
1 tablespoon curry paste
1 teaspoon tandoori paste

Scones *makes 10 scones*
200 g self-raising flour
half a teaspoon salt
1 teaspoon baking powder
40 g butter
150 ml milk

Apple crumble *serves 6 people*
3 large cooking apples
150 g sugar
pinch of cinnamon
200 g flour
100 g butter

Jam sandwich cake *makes 1 cake*
175 g butter
175 g caster sugar
3 eggs
175 g self raising flour
jam

A1 Look at the recipe for pizza topping. It makes topping for 1 pizza.
Jane makes topping for 3 pizzas.

(a) How many onions will she need?

(b) How many grams of parmesan cheese will she need?

A2 The recipe for jam sandwich cake makes 1 cake.

(a) How many eggs do you need for 5 cakes?

(b) How much butter do you need for 2 cakes?

A3 The pumpkin soup recipe makes soup for 2 people.

(a) You need 300 grams of pumpkin for 2 people.
How many grams do you need for 1 person?

(b) How many grams of pumpkin do you need for 4 people?

(c) How much butter do you need to make soup for 6 people?

(d) How much milk do you need for 10 people?

A4 Look at the recipe for scones.

(a) How much flour is there in 1 scone?

(b) How much flour would you need to make 4 scones?

(c) Sandy wants to make 5 scones.

   (i) How much butter does she need?

   (ii) How much flour does she need?

(d) Chloe is making 20 scones.
How much milk will she use?

A5 Look at the recipe for apple crumble.

Use the recipe to copy and complete
this card for apple crumble.

> **Apple crumble** *serves ... people*
> ... large cooking apples
> ... grams sugar
> ... pinches of cinnamon
> ... grams flour
> 200 grams butter

A6 Robert is making jam sandwich cakes.
He has lots of butter, caster sugar, flour and jam but only 12 eggs.
How many cakes can he make?

A7 Rachel is making pancakes.
She has 1 kilogram of plain flour, and lots of the other ingredients.
How many pancakes can she make?

B Making and sharing

B1 This tells you what you need to make fruit punch.
Jess uses one litre of orange squash.

(a) How much lime cordial does she need?

(b) How much lemonade does she need?

(c) How many litres of fruit punch
does she make altogether?

> **Fruit punch**
> Mix one part orange squash,
> one part lime cordial and
> two parts lemonade.

B2 David makes fruit punch using 3 litres of orange squash.

(a) How much of the other ingredients does he need?

(b) How many litres of fruit punch does he make altogether?

B3 Andy and Ben are sharing some stamps.
For every 1 stamp that Andy gets, Ben gets 2.
How many stamps will Ben get if Andy gets 15 stamps?

B4 Amy and Becky are sharing out some sweets.
For every 2 sweets that Amy gets, Becky gets 3.

(a) How many sweets will Becky get if Amy gets

    (i) 4   (ii) 10   (iii) 12

(b) How many sweets will Amy get if Becky gets

    (i) 12   (ii) 30   (iii) 24

What progress have you made?

Statement	Evidence

I can solve simple ratio problems.

> **Gooseberry jam**   makes 10 jars
> 2 kg gooseberries
> 3 kg sugar
> 1 litre water

1 Leah has 6 kg of gooseberries and wants to
make gooseberry jam.

(a) How many jars can she make?

(b) How much sugar will she need?

2 Max wants to make 50 jars of gooseberry
jam. Write out what he needs.

Review 5

1 What number does each arrow point to?

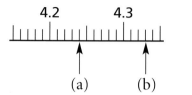 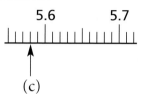 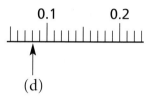

2 Gareth is 167 cm tall. Rachel is 1 m 8 cm tall.
Who is taller? By how many centimetres?

3 Write these lengths in order, shortest first.

1.5 m   128 cm   1.09 m   1 m 1 cm   1.10 m

4 Do these in your head.
   (a) Add a hundredth to 234.56   (b) Add $\frac{1}{10}$ to 234.56
   (c) Add a ten to 234.56   (d) Add a hundred to 234.56

5 Spell a word by arranging the numbers in order, smallest first.

Z	U	P	L	N	I	G	Z
0.1	0.08	0.03	0.18	0.3	0.2	0.35	0.13

6 Here are some items at a greengrocer's.

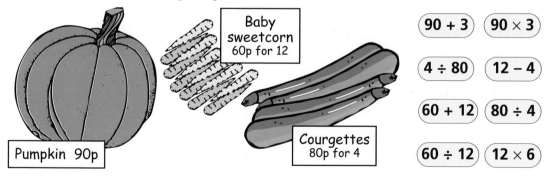

Which of the calculations goes with each of these questions?
   (a) What do 3 pumpkins cost?
   (b) What is the cost of one courgette?
   (c) How many baby sweetcorn are there in 6 packets?
   (d) Amanda buys a packet of baby sweetcorn. She uses 4 of them.
        How many does she have left?

7 This graph shows the number of customers in Melanie's Café one day.

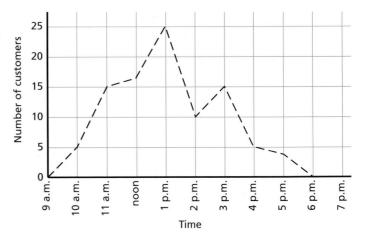

(a) How many customers were there at 9 a.m.?

(b) How many customers were there at 11 a.m.?

(c) (i) At what time were there most customers?

    (ii) Why do you think that was?

(d) What time do you think the café closes?

8 The data set shows the number of birds seen each day on a bird table in February.
Show the data in a frequency bar chart.
A suitable tally chart is started for you.

40	15	35	44	4	9	17
50	23	33	7	10	18	55
38	40	29	11	7	20	38
13	23	42	39	22	51	48

Number of birds	Tally	Frequency
0–9		
10–19		
20–		

9 This table shows the dawn temperature in Seville in the first 10 days of March.
Draw a line graph to show the data.
Make your across axis go from 0 to 10, and your vertical one from 0 to 20.

Day	1	2	3	4	5	6	7	8	9	10
Temperature (°C)	2	5	0	12	10	18	16	11	5	8

10 Work out these in your head.

(a) $\frac{1}{2}$ of 12   (b) $\frac{1}{2}$ of 30   (c) $\frac{1}{3}$ of 24   (d) $\frac{1}{4}$ of 24   (e) $\frac{1}{5}$ of 35

(f) $\frac{1}{3}$ of 15   (g) $\frac{2}{3}$ of 15   (h) $\frac{1}{5}$ of 30   (i) $\frac{2}{5}$ of 30   (j) $\frac{3}{5}$ of 30

11 Harry is 12 years old and 150 cm tall.
Harriet is half as old and $\frac{2}{3}$ as tall.
How old and how tall is Harriet?

12 Which of these pentominoes can be folded up into an open cube?

A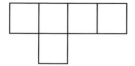

B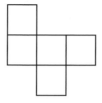

C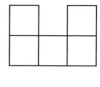

D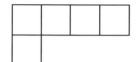

E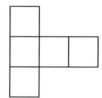

F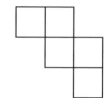

13 Three of these drawings are of the same shape.
Which is the odd one out?

P   Q 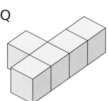 R 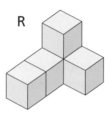 S

14 This recipe makes 10 chocolate brownies.

(a) Mel wants to make 20 brownies.

(i) How much butter does he need?

(ii) How much chocolate should he use?

(iii) How many eggs will he need?

(b) Jan is making 5 brownies.

(i) How much sugar will she need?

(ii) How much flour will she need?

(c) (i) How much sugar do you need to make 1 brownie?

(ii) How much sugar would you need for 8 brownies?

(d) Yann buys a 1 kg packet of flour.
He makes 40 brownies.
How much flour is left in the packet?

Chocolate Brownies   makes 10
100 g butter
75 g chocolate
100 g flour
1 teaspoon baking powder
100 g chopped hazelnuts
200 g sugar
3 eggs

The following are general review questions.

15 Without using a calculator, work out each of these.

    (a) 567 + 173   (b) 632 − 288   (c) £2.66 + 45p   (d) £3 − £1.55

    (e) 243 × 8   (f) 53 × 34   (g) 45 ÷ 8   (h) 442 ÷ 3

16 Without a calculator, work out these.

    (a) 4.7 + 1.6   (b) 8 − 3.4   (c) 3.8 × 4   (d) 146 ÷ 10

17 Without a calculator, work out the cost of these.

    (a) 6 chews which cost 14p each.   (b) 16 books which cost £21 each.

    (c) A flower, if 12 flowers cost 84p.   (d) A magazine, if 16 of them cost £64.

18 (a) Copy the diagram on to centimetre squared paper.

    (b) Write down the coordinates of A, B and C.

    (c) On your diagram, plot the point D at (5, 1).

    (d) Two sides of shape ABCD are parallel. Which sides are they?

    (e) On your diagram, draw in any lines of symmetry which shape ABCD has.

    (f) Measure the length of the side BC in cm.

    (g) What is the perimeter of shape ABCD?

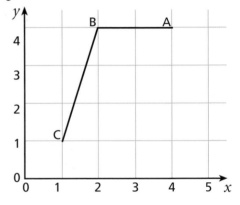

19 Round 4882

    (a) to the nearest 10   (b) to the nearest 100   (c) to the nearest 1000

20 Read this entry from Guérin's diary and then answer the questions below.

> I got up at a quarter to 7 and it was ⁻5°C. Brrrr! When I had lunch (at half past 12) the temperature was 8°C. Much better. But at tea-time at 5:15 p.m. it was back down to ⁻2°C. Tea took 20 minutes and afterwards I went skating for an hour and a half!

    (a) How long was it between when Guérin got up and when he had lunch?

    (b) By how much did the temperature rise from when Guérin got up to lunch-time?

    (c) How long was it between lunch-time and tea-time?

    (d) What was the difference in temperature between lunch-time and tea-time?

    (e) At what time did Guérin finish skating?

21 What fraction of each tile is red?
What fraction is yellow?

(a) 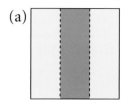 (b) 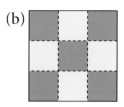 (c) 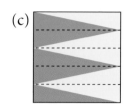 (d)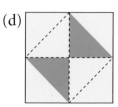

22 Work out the missing numbers.
Write down each rule for working them out.

(a) 2, 6, 10, 14, 18, 22, ..., ...

(b) 65, 62, 59, 56, 53, 50, ..., ...

(c) 0.5, 0.7, 0.9, 1.1, 1.3, 1.5, ..., ...

(d) 500, 530, 560, 590, 620, 650, ..., ...

23 Which event goes with which arrow on the probability line?

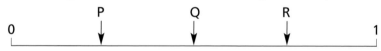

(a) Getting an odd number when you roll a dice

(b) Getting a heart when you take a card from a pack

(c) Not getting a heart when you take a card from a pack

24 (a) Draw this shape accurately.

(b) Measure the side CD.

(c) Work out the perimeter of the shape.

(d) Does the shape have any lines of symmetry?
If so, draw any that it has.

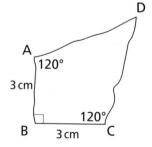

25 Without using a calculator, work these out.

(a) $4 \times (5 - 2)$ (b) $4 \times 5 - 2$ (c) $24 \div 4 - 2$ (d) $24 \div (4 - 2)$

(e) $32 + 8 \div 4$ (f) $(32 + 8) \div 4$ (g) $20 - 6 - 2$ (h) $20 - (6 - 2)$

26 Find the missing number in each of these.

(a) $10 + (\blacklozenge - 3) = 15$ (b) $2 \times (\blacktriangledown + 1) = 12$ (c) $3 \times \blacktriangle + 6 = 12$

(d) $6 + \blacksquare \times 2 = 14$ (e) $18 - \ast \div 2 = 8$ (f) $\blacktriangledown + 5 \times 2 = 20$

Index